Computers in Curriculum and Instruction

Edited by M. Tim Grady and Jane D. Gawronski

Editing:
Ronald S. Brandt, ASCD Executive Editor
Nancy Carter Modrak, Managing Editor, Booklets

Cover design:
Congressional Arts

ASCD Stock Number: 611-83292
ISBN: 0-87120-116-X
Library of Congress Card Catalog Number: 82-073969

Contents

Foreword

By the turn of the century, most Americans will never have known a world without silicon chips. Those of us who do remember a world without computers will undoubtedly marvel at the dramatic changes wrought in our personal lives—all because of an electrical current transported across millions of microscopic wafers fabricated from sand.

The silicon chip has already brought computers out of the mystery of remote (psychologically if not physically) computation centers and into our homes, offices, and schools via microcomputer terminals. Our language has welcomed a freshet of once arcane words like "byte," "interface," "modem," "BASIC," and, yes, "chips." And words like "menu," "memory," "program," and "friendly" have been invested with new meanings. Friends with personal micros (we easily shorten words in familiarity) use them to maintain personal records, pay bills, monitor their homes' energy use, write letters, play games, plan budgets, update their Christmas card lists, and more. At some schools, pupils lug their own micros to class and back home at night. Most schools have at least one micro (if only to assert respectability), and some have a number of micros in use throughout the day.

Still, many schools are not using microcomputers at all, and most of us educators are not yet literate or even comfortable with them. Few of us own a micro, even though one may be high on our personal wish list.

This book, then, is for educators who are taking those first steps to purchase and use computers in school. It is for educators like me—individuals who are interested in computers, who do not own one, who are largely nonliterate about them, and who recognize the obvious benefits of computer use in education and personal living. This book is a guide to beginning.

I have found it informative. More, it has stimulated my imagination. I am confident that it will fill a unique position in our work and thinking.

Our Association is deeply indebted to Tim Grady. A pioneer in the use of computers in classrooms, he has a rich curriculum and computer science background. His leadership has integrated microcomputer technology into the operations of a local school district. Additionally, he has helped educators across the nation to become "friendly" with computers.

Grady planned this book and invited Jane Gawronski to join him as editor. Together they assembled a group of contributors whose knowledge and competence is confirmed throughout the book. I am pleased to extend our Association's thanks to each of them.

We will all use this book.

Oh, yes—I must get on to my appointment at my local microcomputer store. I'm nearing a decision about which microcomputer I should buy!

O. L. Davis, Jr.
President, 1982–83
Association for Supervision
and Curriculum Development

Introduction

THE INFLUENCE OF COMPUTER TECHNOLOGY ON EDUCATION has been and will continue to be felt at all levels. The very teaching/learning process itself, as well as the context in which teaching and learning occur, is enhanced by the use of computers and computer-related technologies.

Considering the nature of contemporary curricula and the accessibility of computer technology, it appears that both the content and methodologies of education are changing, especially in mathematics and communications. Communication skills affected include reading, writing, and speaking, and emphasize knowing how to use both numeric and bibliographic data bases. Especially important is the ability to know what data need to be collected and, once collected, how to analyze, store, retrieve, manipulate, manage, and control information, as well as to make decisions and predictions based on it.

These skills are particularly pressing right now in vocational education. According to the 13th Annual Gallup Poll, 56 percent of parents indicated that schools were not spending enough time preparing students for jobs and careers after high school graduation. In addition, American work patterns have changed dramatically over the past 30 years. In 1950, 17 percent of the work force was in information-related occupations, as opposed to 55 percent in 1980. Thus, restructuring curricular content and methodology is essential if we are to provide students with experiences that will help them cope with the roles of today, as well as develop enough flexibility to obtain the new skills required for tomorrow.

Schools are buying computers and software for both instructional and administrative purposes. As their program funds decrease, schools tend to put their money into capital outlay rather than into recurring personnel costs, for good reason. Consider, for example, a school that spends $2,000 for a microcomputer with a life span of several years. Had the school instead spent that $2,000 on the services of a paraprofessional for one year, the next year it would cost at least another $2,000 to buy the same services once again. Since schools have no assurance that funds will continue at the same level, some are looking at computer technology as a way of helping them provide programs that

vii

are machine related, or facilitated by hardware and software, and which are not as dependent on personnel or as labor intensive.

Decisions to buy computers in school districts are ultimately made at the superintendent or assistant superintendent level. However, the initial decision influencer, or prime mover, in the decision is most often the teacher or building principal. It is in the school that personnel see the immediate need for computers, and it is the classroom teacher who, once computers are acquired, is most influential and critical to their successful use. Inservice and preservice programs must emphasize providing computer literacy experiences for teachers to ensure that this success does, in fact, happen.

Most schools will certainly have computers and computer literacy instruction by 1985. Already such instruction can be found in available materials. In the long run, however, we will not need separate courses in computer literacy; it will have become an integral part of our instruction in communication, information processing, mathematics. But for now, we must build computer literacy training into preservice programs in teacher education and in workshops and inservice provided by county offices or other regional agencies. Another source for literacy training is the computer vendors themselves in their learning centers.

One problem that schools face is the lack of comprehensive instructional materials in computer technology for students. Currently available materials are piecemeal; they're good supplemental support materials, but they are not comprehensive and they lack the scope and sequence that relate to present or new curricula.

We need at least two kinds of materials. One is for the student market—materials that integrate computer literacy concepts and computer programming into the ongoing curriculum. The other is teacher training materials to acquaint teachers with strategies for teaching about and using computers in their classrooms. If teachers from the same building are trained together, they can, in fact, support each other's efforts. This idea of peer or collegial support is critical since it is adults who have expressed fear of computers or resistance to them. This same kind of fear or resistance doesn't exist among adolescents. Where computers have been placed in instructional media centers, students have virtually taught themselves how to load and use canned programs and have gone on to teach themselves BASIC. Students, however, still need materials that teach them that they run the machine, the machine doesn't run them. Materials must also be teacher-free to the extent that students, once motivated and familiar with what needs to be done, can then use the materials with a minimum of teacher intervention.

The ideal computer literacy teaching environment would give every student a microcomputer, one transportable from school to home to "public access learning environments" and capable of interfacing with television networks. We would be able to monitor learning experiences both in school and out of school. The use of inexpensive micros assigned on an individual basis to students would then result in truly individualized instruction.

The purpose of this booklet is to introduce school administrators to the use of computers, to identify sources of information, and to determine ways to implement and monitor effective use of computers. Curriculum applications, histories of successful programs, and strategies for staff development are also included. These are meant to guide, encourage, and provide the reader with motivation and ability to learn even more about computers' uses for educators.

J. D. Gawronski
Director
Planning, Research and Evaluation
San Diego County Department of Education
San Diego, California

I. Planning for Computers

1. Computers in the 80's

Charlene E. West

DURING THIS DECADE, COMPUTERS WILL BEGIN TO INFLUENCE every aspect of our daily lives. Already advanced technology is evident in offices, factories, schools, and homes. Visibly and invisibly, computers are shaping society. Most of us can't go through a single day without coming in contact with some form of advanced technology—whether buying groceries, ordering a Big Mac, making travel reservations, diagnosing what's wrong with our cars, or searching for a new home to live in. Perhaps most important, micro-electronics has made it possible for many of us to have our own computer at home. This is just the beginning.

Because of advanced technology, we will be experiencing major changes in our personal lives during the 1980s. By the end of the decade, one in every three Americans will have their own computer and/or terminal. Intelligent credit cards will be available within the next year (wallet size plastic cards with a built-in microprocessor to be used as substitutes for travelers checks). By 1985 most company mail will be received electronically and users will get printouts only of the most pertinent information. Coin-operated computers will be available for use in public places, just as copying machines are today. Electronic newspapers already are beginning to appear in major cities. Shopping at home via TV will become commonplace. Many new developments are predicted in the areas of speech recognition, speech synthesis, worldwide video telephone systems, bookless libraries, and teacherless schools. Already available is an electronic encyclopedia that can be updated daily.

Today more than half of the jobs in the nation are in the information industry. A study carried out by the U.S. Department of Labor Statistics shows that of the ten fastest growing jobs during the 1980s,

2

three out of the top five are in the computer industry. Over three-fourths of today's kindergarten students will one day be employed in occupations requiring computer literacy.

These statistics have placed a real burden on American educators. In fact, both the National Institute of Education and the National Science Foundation have identified the next crisis in education to be that of computer illiteracy. We must begin to help our students overcome their ignorance of technology.

The prospect for the future is a dramatic change in the way we educate our students. The days of the little red schoolhouse, textbooks, and conventional 30-student classrooms may be numbered. The new technology offers the possibility of truly individualized instruction tailored to fit the special needs of each student. Computers in the classroom will be used as (1) the object of instruction—computer literacy; (2) the medium of instruction—computer-assisted instruction (CAI), simulations, problem solving; and (3) the manager of instruction—recordkeepers, test scorers, and prescribers of instruction. The computer will be used as a tool much as the calculator has been since the 1970s. With the computer to perform mathematical calculations and organize and display data, students can focus on the task of problem solving.

Computer languages are also being developed to fit users' needs. Some of the commonly used microcomputer languages include (1) BASIC, the original microcomputer language; (2) PASCAL, a structured computer language; (3) PILOT, designed for those who write computer-assisted instruction; (4) LOGO, an easy language for children that gives them control over the machine; and (5) various author languages designed to help teachers write their own CAI programs. By 1990, teachers will be able to "talk" to computers, who will write their own programs.

With the decrease in cost and increase in availability of the microcomputer, formal education will reach far more people than ever before. Adults, with computers available in their homes, will continue their educations throughout life. Education will also change dramatically for handicapped individuals, and businesses will be able to use microcomputers for specific on-the-job training.

New input/output devices, such as speech synthesis, touch display screens, musical keyboards, and keys coded with colors and symbols, enable educators to work with preschool children using computers. Preschoolers seem to enjoy interacting with computers because of their game-like attraction. The next few years will see more experimentation with computers and preschoolers in hand-eye coordination, increased pre-reading readiness, and elimination of sex stereotyping in various subject areas (such as females and math phobia).

As computer technology develops, new, heretofore unthinkable applications become possible. The ability to communicate with the computer through speech is becoming a reality. Although still in its infancy, voice recognition and synthesis is beginning to develop rapidly. The possibilities afforded by this development are almost limitless. Computers that people can talk to and that can talk back will be perceived as "friendly" machines; people will be less fearful of computers. When used in industry, these tools will increase efficiency by freeing personnel to do other tasks concurrently and aiding the problem-solving process by communicating through speech rather than by conventional means. This technology shows promise of transforming the lives of the visually handicapped. A new device, the Kurzweil reading machine, scans a printed page, stores it in memory, and converts the information to spoken words. By using a voice synthesizer, the machine is able to communicate with the blind. Advanced technology is also affecting the education of the deaf with computers and videodiscs.

The introduction of the television in the classroom failed to make a major impact on the instructional process because television was a virtually passive medium. Today, with the help of advanced technology, instructional television has become an interactive medium. We are now experimenting with teletext systems to transmit pages of information that are decoded and presented on a TV screen. These systems can be used in schools with instructional television for testing and reinforcement. Since there are over 1,000 data bases available to the public, the 1980s will see schools, offices, and homes using these teletext systems for national and international news, weather, stock market information, banking, and shopping. Daily electronic newsletters will be available to educators. It will be possible to send coded emergency information to schools, civil defense centers, police stations, hospitals—anywhere—using teletext systems. As energy costs rise during the 80s, we will see more and more workers doing their work at home and communicating with others via teletext, computers, and teleconferencing.

One of the most exciting new technologies to be available to education in recent years is the videodisc. With the videodisc, not only can students view a program straight through, they can view it in slow motion, and even hold a frame if necessary. This allows the machine to be a very effective teaching tool, particularly for slow learners. But the real potential of the videodisc is when it is combined with a microcomputer to produce an interactive learning experience. This system will move on to new material if the student answers the questions correctly, and can branch to a section on remediation if the student answers the question incorrectly. It can analyze incorrect responses and determine appropriate types of remediation.

Some schools have already begun to use the videodisc systems. The most innovative is perhaps the California School for the Deaf where the videodisc is used with an Apple II computer to teach reading and language development.

Videodiscs or their next generation counterpart will probably be standard school equipment by 1989. Students may even be able to revise, rearrange, and annotate conceptual material via a built-in editing system. Suppose, in viewing a lesson, that you wanted to make notes to yourself about important concepts. With a built-in editing system, you could do that right on the videodisc. Then, when reviewing the lesson, your own notes would also be on the disc.

Unfortunately, because of a lack of good software, many schools are simply using the videodisc to replace the film projector rather than using it in innovative ways. Software designed specifically for the schools is beginning to appear and, in two or three years, should be available in many curriculum areas. The videodisc may revolutionize education by providing a medium where students can interact and be provided with instant, individualized access to frames of learning.

More and more educators are becoming involved in the new technology. In fact, some universities are developing courses in instructional technology. With this involvement will hopefully come the much-needed quality software and courseware that will make technology a reality in every classroom. We are looking forward to the 80s as the decade of the new technology.

2. Computer and Other Literacies

Ramon Zamora

ABOUT TWENTY YEARS AGO, EDUCATORS EARNESTLY DEBATED THE LIKELY impacts of computers on schools. As the debate progressed, a generation of kids grew up and invented much of today's technology. In particular, they helped create the microcomputer, a tool that already promises to alter how we learn and teach.

Twenty years from now, the children using today's technologies will create tomorrow's information tools. In the interim, a new debate arises over what we should teach the current crop of future-makers with and about computers.

Teach With Or Teach About?

As Marshall McLuhan pointed out, computers are not part of the "Gutenberg technology." They are not new kinds of "engines." Computers are open-ended, nonlinear extensions of our "central nervous systems," and as such the uses of computers can produce nonlinear results.

The influence of computers and informational technologies on education and our culture cannot be predicted simply. Attempts to define "computer literacy" are attempts to capture organic, nonlinear phenomena in a linear format. Definitions are, by definition, restrictive. They exclude, narrow, and ultimately stop people from thinking. They can also create confusion when everyone's definition is different.

The value of definitions, however, especially divergent ones, is that all the points of view taken together can provide a look at the whole. Two such emergent observations come from aggregating the variety of computer literacy definitions to yield:

(a) Computer literacy deals with a spectrum of computer users, users' needs, and delivery systems.

(b) The spectrum can be naturally divided into two areas dealing with learning *with* computers and learning *about* computers.

The spectrum of users ranges from the truly "naive" person (perhaps someone who doesn't know computers exist) to the people designing the technology; that is, nearly everybody on the planet. Their needs encompass virtually all applications of the technology that enhance productivity, efficiency, education, recreation, and personal growth. Formal and informal delivery systems can be based in classrooms, storefronts, libraries, museums, homes, and businesses. The systems rely on multi-media materials to deliver content.

People have tried to break up this huge grouping by developing targeted computer literacy activities and materials for subgroups within the spectrum. Titles such as "Computer Comfort," "Computer Awareness," "Computer Programming," "Computers in the Schools," "Computer Languages," "Computers and Math," "Computer Design," and "Recreational Uses of Computers" suggest the proliferation taking place.

Is this approach to computer literacy workable? Partially, and the task is monumental and possibly doomed by changes that will take place in the technology and the culture. In addition, part of the confusion as to what directions and positions educators should take regarding the use of computers becomes masked by the sheer magnitude of dealing with the subject in this way.

The question of whether we want to teach a subject *with* the computer, teach people *about* the computer, or do both makes for a simple place to start. In fact, applying this observation backwards to the first observation begins to simplify the difficulties of the broad goal of giving many people the opportunity to use the technology. Stated briefly, do we want a nation of people who know the uses of the computer or who know about the computer?

Other questions come to mind. Is there actually a *difference* in teaching the uses of computers and the use of a computer? Do the newer languages (LOGO, PILOT, Smalltalk) create a third class of activities: *teaching the computer?* Where should educators begin? Much of this book provides information upon which to build answers. A word of caution is in order, though: everything is changing, and changing quickly. Today's answer might be tomorrow's dead end. Much of the debate centers on a technology and marketplace reaction that is only a few years old. The press of events requires current action tempered by the experiences with this technology to date.

Knowing Computers, Or Knowing Computer Uses?

When computers first came to be, people spent a lot of time learning about the computer. The uses of the computer, the applications, were limited and restricted to what the computer's inventors wanted done.

Over the past twenty years, the number of applications for computers has increased and larger numbers of nontechnical people have used computers to perform routine tasks. Computers can be found in a multitude of business, household, and personal devices. Even toys contain computers. Millions of people now have access to microcomputers. Each microcomputer supports hundreds, if not thousands, of applications. Most individuals end up knowing something about the computer; many, however, know more of the uses of the tool than about the tool itself.

If we roughly map the present trend, we might take three snapshots in time on the relationships between users and computers. In the past, interaction with a computer was dominated by how much the user knew about the computer. Today, in order to be productive, people do not appear to need detailed knowledge of the computers they use— which has implications for the trend in the future. Apparently, we are moving toward knowing less about computers and more about their uses.

As computers become integrated into our work and lives, there is no clear evidence that the word "computer" will survive. Increasingly, we use the applications that make our efforts more productive and enjoyable. We don't use the computer; we make use of it through its applications.

Delivery Systems

The computer came to us as a room filled with tubes and wires. Over time, the computer processing unit shrank until it fit on a small chip whose details are visible through a microscope. Some peripheral devices that make it useful to us (keyboards, printers, tape units, disk drives, screens) have been tailored to give us a "personal" computer. We can now put a computer on the corner of our desk or in our pocket. The "box" that contains the computer continues to change, adapting itself to our needs.

The systems for learning about computers have also changed. Technical journals and research publications contained the first information on computers and computing. Industry, governments, and universities developed most of the early computers. Eventually, as the

size and cost of computers dropped, lay publications appeared, targeted for the nontechnical user. Currently, an unprecedented flood of
books, magazines, newsletters, and audio/video materials appears side-
by-side with microcomputers. Formal and informal educational activities about and with microcomputers are everywhere. Instruction with
or about microcomputers occurs on all age levels from child to senior
citizen.

Communications technologies indicate that soon anyone will be
able to send and receive information from anywhere on the planet at
times that fit their convenience. Distance and time collapse into
McLuhan's "Global Village." We are everywhere at all times.

We can learn, work, and play electronically while at home, the
office, in the car, or riding on public transit. The office can be
anywhere; school can be anywhere. Also, the nature of the combined
tools, computers and communications, points toward a "personal"
electronic or information environment. We can select our informational "reality" from the immense sea of commercial and public offerings.

Work or Play?

Early computers worked for a living. Many of today's computers
entertain for a living. The low-cost microprocessor chip has found a
home in the major entertainment technologies: televisions, stereos,
toys, video tape recorders, videodisc players, and hosts of similar
products. The marriage of the computer and the television spawned
video games, a precursor of the entertainment media of the future.

Work and learning can benefit from the spillover from the entertainment areas. A small collection of business products now use color
and sound to augment the display of information. Teleconferencing
(business as theater) is widely available. Experimental "learning stations" that contain a number of "invisible" computers are being tested
on preschool children and servicemen aboard submarines. The learning stations combine the technologies and disciplines of the computer,
video, communications, brain research, psychology, and creative design, or produce "learning environments." Adaptations of these environments as components of a new form of participatory, public
"teaching" are being explored.

The highly interactive nature of combined technologies points to a
future where work, learning, and entertainment seem to meld, and
where the richness of the entertainment area pervades other activities.
In the future (to paraphrase McLuhan), those of us who make a
distinction between learning and recreation will not know much about
either.

Other Literacies

Computer literacy, as a point of discussion, is going to be short-lived. The predictions outlined here indicate the forces that are pushing us on to the ultimate opportunities that the computer is creating for us. Widespread use of microcomputers continues to spawn innovations that promise to subsume their progenitor. New technologies appear daily.

Is "technological literacy" then the subject of the next great debate? Possibly, if people choose to generate that discussion. Ultimately, it too would be included in a much broader conversation. The fundamental unit of analysis that underpins nearly every attempt to define literacy activities (technological, computer, scientific, political, economic, and so forth) is one of *information*.

The need to process large mathematical computations drove the development of the early computers. In those cases, *information*, in terms of mathematics, provided the stimulus for experimenting with alternate technical solutions. In the last decade, the amount of information available and accessible to the average person increased dramatically. The increase took place in all areas and involved all disciplines. Electronic communication channels helped disperse and distribute information around the globe. Technology now allows us to carry the contents of a library under our arm.

Our children are growing up in an information-rich environment; rich almost to the point of overwhelm. Information flows around and through us, can be picked out of the air and brought into our proximity at the touch of a dial or push of a button. Today's children progress toward a future where accessing, creating, and manipulating information products and services will be essential skills.

One of the best preparations for that future would be to focus on information literacy, not on narrowly defined concepts of computer or technological literacy. On the way, people may need to learn the uses of a computer, to use a computer, and perhaps even something about the computer. The computer, however, is not the goal but the tool. The goal is the development of empowered and fully functional citizens of an information-based society.

Since our children already own the future, what, then, is our role? We can only assist them as they take control.

Bibliography

Johnson, David C., and others. "Computer Literacy—What Is It?" *Mathematics Teacher* (February 1980): 91–96.

Leuhrmann, Arthur. "Computer Literacy—What Should It Be?" *Mathematics Teacher* (February 1981): 682–690.

McLuhan, Marshall, and Fiore, Q. *War and Peace in the Global Village.* New York: Bantam Books, 1968.

Moursand, David. *Precollege Computer Literacy: A Personal Approach.* Eugene, Oregon: Internatinoal Council for Computers in Education, 1981.

Papert, Seymour. *Mindstorms.* New York: Basic Books, 1980.

Taylor, R. P. *The Computer in the School: Tutor, Tool, Tutee.* New York: Teachers College Press, 1980.

3. Research on School Computing

Karen Billings

HISTORICALLY, THE LITERATURE REGARDING THE EFFECTIVENESS OF COMPUTER use has been concerned with achievement gains through computer-assisted instruction (CAI). Typically, large-scale studies have examined the results of computer programs written for mainframe or minicomputers. Generally, these studies have been in the subjects of mathematics and language arts.

More recently, studies of computer use have looked at the formation of computer literacy skills, programming environments, and problem-solving strategies. Other studies have looked at the computer's effectiveness as a tool for learning computation or writing.

CAI Studies in General

Many reviews have been done on the impact of CAI on achievement and secondary education. Vinsonhaler and Bass (1972) reviewed the major studies on CAI drill and practice at the elementary level. They found that augmenting classroom instruction with CAI provides superior performance on the SAT. Other reviews of the literature (Burns and Culp, 1980; Johnson and Jongejan, 1981) support the notion that supplementary instruction with CAI leads to higher achievement and that the amount of time needed to learn is significantly reduced for mathematics or language arts skills.

Johnson and Jongejan (1981), through computer searches of data banks, summarized research in an unpublished appendix to a report on computers and mathematics for the Association of Computing Machinery. In reviewing the research on the effects of drill and practice, they found "that the style of computer usage to present a stimulus (question) and review and evaluate a response (answer) has generally been successful."

This review was concerned primarily with elementary school mathematics, but does include several secondary and higher education studies. In studies done primarily with college students, Johnson and Jongejan (1981) found that "Curriculum developers have generally used the format of programmed texts to direct their computer delivered curriculum . . . results of these efforts have been similar to the more traditional programmed texts; that is, sometimes positive, sometimes negative."

Regarding simulation studies with predominantly college level students, they said, "Efforts to utilize the computer to simulate some complex models have been very successful. Translating these simulations into productive instructional activities has been effective too."

Similarly, they summarized that "Instructional activities delivered by a computer have required less time for students to complete than a similar activity delivered by other means." When looking at the results of studies of the effect of computer-delivered instruction on the attitudes of students, they concluded that "Results . . . have been mixed but generally show the attitude is maintained or increased."

Johnson and Jongejan also summarized the works on the impact of using computers to manage information about students and their instructional progress. In general, they concluded that computers are "very effective." They reviewed studies that reported improved record-keeping and student progress logs. Only in a study involving behaviorally disordered students was achievement increased.

A study by HumRRO for the Office of Technology Assessment reviewed 32 studies in simulation and adaptive testing. The majority of these studies showed savings in the learner's time to complete a course of study, greater efficiency in terms of achievement per unit of time, improved skills, and the provision of instruction not previously available by conventional methods. HumRRO's review leads to the conclusion that computer-based education can be an improvement over conventional methods.

Computers and Problem Solving

The Johnson and Jongejan review (1981) indicated that students of all ages have been taught programming skills and asked to use these skills to solve problems. The results of their studies, which compare problem solving using the computer to traditional problem-solving instruction, generally favored the computer. They noted, however, that high ability students seemed to profit more.

Research conducted by Foster (1973) showed that 8th grade students using a computer to solve mathematical problems out-performed the group using no computers and the groups using flowcharts only. Johnson and Harding (Birmingham Lea Writing Group, 1979), in a United Kingdom study, found that "students who studied mathematics with computing are more apt to employ different problem-solving strategies effectively and/or perform significantly better on mathematical problem-solving tasks."

Project SOLO at the University of Pittsburgh was designed to offer an environment for teaching general problem-solving strategies. Principal investigator Thomas Dwyer argued that computers provide the vehicle for a learning style with powerful motivational and cognitive effects if students develop SOLO ability at programming and then apply their ability to challenging, interdisciplinary problems. The project reports are primarily descriptive narratives of the types of projects completed by pupils. They provide case study data that indicate "pupils are able to attack (albeit, research) a wide variety of interesting problems which involve the application and/or extension of the mathematics they have been studying."

Computers and Writing

Research on the computer as a writing tool is recent and suggests that CAI and word processing packages may play an important role in the writing process. Researchers have hypothesized and studied the effects of using the computer in both the composing and revising steps.

Burns and Culp (1980) asked if supplementary computer-assisted instruction could be effective at stimulating an individual's inventive process. They designed, programmed, tested, and evaluated three CAI modules to simulate rhetorical invention within a freshman English composition setting.

Dialog models of question-answering systems were designed for the computer. These became the tutoring device to help students explore a topic at the pre-writing stage. The program, known as generative CAI, interacts with and prompts the user, emulating the verbal behavior of intelligent, inquisitive, human tutors. After a pilot study and a treatment study involving control and experimental groups, Burns and Culp (1980) found that the experimental group differed significantly from the control group "with respect to the number of ideas generated, the insightfulness and factuality of the ideas, the surface cued intellectual processing evident in the sample writing, as well as overall quality of the inquiry" (p. 9).

Their second important finding was that "computer administered posttest methodology represented a more stringent way for controlling and perhaps later replicating quasi-experimental research in rhetoric" (Burns and Culp, 1980, p. 10). The most beneficial consequence of the study was perhaps the "introduction of the computer as a way to increase the reliability and the validity of composition research."

The study also contributed "some evidence that the three heuristic strategies via CAI are better than what little individualized invention actually occurs in the composition classroom; at least as far as quantity, comprehensiveness, intellectual processing, and overall quality of ideas are concerned" (Burns and Culp, 1980).

Other researchers have asked questions about the revision process in writing. Does the computer text editor help children who have trouble revising their own writing? Do the capabilities of word processors or related utility programs reduce the physical and cognitive burdens of revising?

A research project entitled "The Effects of Automatic Prompting on Young Writers" (Daiute, 1981) adapted a text-editing program and studied characteristic error patterns in the writing of 4th to 8th graders. The students in the pilot study used the computer as a tool to find out "whether a writing instrument that is interactive stimulates revising and whether the relatively simple error identification and prompts can draw children into the text sufficiently so they do more revising than they do with paper and pencil." They wrote and tested a program to teach children to touch type. Most of the subjects mastered the program in a few hours and enjoyed using it. At least half of the subjects transferred their touch-typing skills to typing for writing. The children found writing on the computer easier than writing by hand, and they wrote more willingly. They also enjoyed making changes in their texts and learned to make more types of revisions.

Action Research

Action or informal research has been reported in newsletters and popular magazines that deal with immediate questions about microcomputer use. This type of research is usually case study or narrative in style with results that convey impressions and feelings. Their value lies in the possibility of the results being shared quickly and easily with others who may be facing the same question. Also, the teacher plays a very active role in the research and benefits directly from it. Hopefully, if enough teachers and practitioners examine the same questions, strong evidence may come out about how microcomputers and students best interact.

Carl Berger at the University of Michigan monitored elementary and junior high students of all ability levels as they worked with a microcomputer program requiring estimation of linear distances. After checking the accuracy of student estimates, the amount of time required for an accurate estimate, and the kind of strategies employed, they did see a drop in time and the development of sound strategies for every student ("Action Research Roundup," 1981).

A 1978 study of 5th and 6th grade high achievers in mathematics at the West Lafayette schools in Indiana showed that access to microcomputers helped children develop problem-solving skills and fostered positive attitudes toward mathematics. Students in the experimental group were given access to calculators and computers and encouraged to use a heuristic approach to problem solving. Students learned BASIC programming skills and were urged to compare and analyze solutions. Although both groups showed progress, the experimental group showed a higher rate of improvement with a test of computation and problem solving as measured by observations and attitude surveys. They found that the experimental group had a higher positive attitude toward mathematics ("Action Research Roundup," 1981).

Pitschka and Wagner worked with 3rd and 4th graders in California to see if microcomputers would help below-grade-level students improve basic skills in mathematics. The study "used pretests and posttests to compare the progress of two groups: one which received daily 15 minute sessions of computer-assisted drill and practice as a supplement to arithmetic studies, and a second which received traditional instruction" ("Action Research Roundup," 1981). Their report indicates that the computer time paid off. The experimental group (computers) scored significantly higher than the control group on the posttest. The average test score of 3.0 (about one year behind grade level) for each group moved to 4.7 and 3.9 respectively.

Computer Games

Computer games have been used to teach traditional content and for entertainment. Is the game format helpful or distracting to the end goals? Why are computer games so intriguing? Will there be harmful effects from the "shoot 'em up" variety such as "Invaders" or other space war games?

The popularity of computer games is obvious to anyone who has wandered through a shopping mall or airport lounge in the last year. Why are these games so captivating? Malone (1980), in his dissertation work at Stanford, systematically studied over 100 people playing with computer games. He found that the characteristics that make instructional environments intrinsically interesting fit into one of three categories: (1) *challenge*—the existence of a goal whose outcome is uncertain but personally meaningful, with a variable difficulty level; (2) *fantasy*—both extrinsic, which depends on the use of the skill, and intrinsic, where problems are presented in terms of fantasy; or (3) *curiosity*—where the environments are novel and surprising. The program may provide a sequence of increasingly complex tasks that are within the learner's ability to grasp.

Computer Implementation

How do school systems assimilate computer innovations to their own values and ways of doing things? How is the impact of technology affecting children, teachers, administrators, and the school system itself?

Sheingold and others (1981) looked at how computer innovations were proceeding in three very different school systems in a large city in the southwest, a smaller midwestern city, and a small northeastern suburb. They used case study methodology and interviewed community residents, school board members, administrators, computer resource personnel, media specialists, teachers and students. They observed students using microcomputers in classrooms, media centers, and resource rooms.

In all sites they found five common problems with computer innovation: (1) differential access to microcomputers; (2) emergence of new ideas among teachers and students; (3) lack of integration of microcomputers into elementary classrooms and the curriculum; (4) inadequate quantity and quality of software; and (5) lack of knowledge of effects and outcomes. Most of the people who were interviewed thought that the computer was having an effect on students. (However, the comments provided anecdotal information rather than research data.)

Summary

The research on the effects of microcomputers, while still not extensive, does provide curriculum workers with positive results on which to base new curricula. The research on the effects of CAI on achievement generally shows significant positive results. Since so few methods studies result in positive effects, we can be encouraged by these findings. The limitations of the existing research is that few subject areas have been included in the studies. We need more serious studies in a variety of subject areas and across a range of grade levels.

We can take hope from the results of the studies on teaching problem solving and composition. More studies need to be made in which more of the salient variables are included; however, there seems to be something about student motivation that is influenced by working with computers in the "creative" aspects of the curriculum. Perhaps there will be more studies on the effects of computers in assisting us to teach problem solving and similar curricula.

Action research conducted by classroom teachers and their supervisors has yielded useful data about the impact of microcomputers in schools. If more research is done collectively, it will yield some consistent results from which we can make meaningful generalizations.

Research findings to date allow us to take heart at the potential value of the computer in areas of skill development, problem-solving skills, writing, and simulations. The jury is still out, however. We need much more systematic research in a variety of subject areas at all levels. As curriculum workers, teachers, and principals begin to use computers in their schools, the data on achievement, motivation, and time variables need to be collected and published for use by the educational community.

References

"Action Research Roundup." *Classroom Computer News* (September–October 1981): 18–20.

Birmingham Lea Writing Group. "Computers in the Classroom." Project Paper 14—Computer in School Mathematics. Chelsen College, University of London, May 1979.

Burns, H. L., and Culp, G. H. "Stimulating Invention in English Composition Through Computer Assisted Instruction." *Educational Technology* (August 1980): 6–10.

Daiute, C. A. "The Effects of Automatic Prompting in Young Writers." First Year Report of the Spencer Foundation, September 1981.

Dwyer, T. *Project SOLO Reports*. Pittsburgh, Penn.: University of Pittsburgh, 1978.

Foster, T. E. "The Effect of Computer Programming Experiences on Student Problem Solving Behaviors in Eighth Grade Mathematics." University of Wisconsin, 1973.

Johnson, J., and Jongejan, T. Unpublished appendix to "Mathematics and Computers" in *Elementary and Secondary School Topics*. Association for Computing Machinery, 1981.

Malone, T. W. "What Makes Things Fun to Learn? A Study of Intrinsically Motivating Computer Games." Technical Report No. CIS-7 (SSL-80-11). Palo Alto, Calif.: Xerox Palo Alto Research Center, 1980.

Sheingold, K.; Kane, J.; Endreweit, M.; and Billings, K. "Issues Related to the Implementation of Computer Technology in Schools: A Cross Sectional Study." Washington, D.C.: National Institute of Education, 1981.

Vinsonhaler, J. F., and Bass, R. K. "A Summary of Ten Major Studies on CAI Drill and Practice." *Educational Technology* (July 1972): 29–32.

Editor's Note:
What We Still Need to Know

MICROCOMPUTERS ARE EVERYWHERE, INCLUDING SCHOOLS, but what educational objectives are attained through their use? Let's look at some research questions worth studying. If we can begin to get some answers to the following questions, then the educational community will be able to plan and implement new computer based curricula from a more knowledgeable position.

Question 1: Motivation

Exactly what is the relationship between students' levels of motivation and their willingness to work with computers? One assertion is that low motivated students are apt to do exercises on the computer that the teacher would not otherwise get them to do. How do we know that this is so? Exactly what kinds of transfer occur? What lasting effects does computer use have on students' ability to "do" mathematics or any other subject? How do we distinguish between a computer lesson that is motivational and one that isn't?

Question 2: Graphics

Has research shown any benefits of graphics—for instance, when used with a mathematics lesson? Some theoreticians say that graphics are actually distracting, which is why language arts courseware, for example, uses very little graphics. Yet, in high school geometry, it would seem that graphics would be helpful, just as pictures in a book are enlightening. The trouble is, we know very little and are therefore relying on opinion for our decisions. In programming courses, many feel the skills needed to program graphics are helpful and transferable to other problems. We need to know if this is true. Much work needs to be done before we can fully understand the benefits and limitations of graphics in CAI and other courseware.

Question 3: Educational Validity

School staff members are frequently frustrated when trying to locate courseware that "runs" on their hardware. Part of the confusion that surrounds many microcomputer projects is the lack of order in the software market. Some software clearinghouse-type projects have been initiated (such as Microsift), but we still have a basic need for some fundamental research to determine whether software packages are educationally valid. That is, does the software do what it is supposed to do?

Question 4: Timing

What is the optimum length for a CAI lesson in remedial mathematics? How long should units last? Or frames? How many questions should a drill sequence contain? Does the use of microcomputers reduce the amount of time needed to acquire a skill or concept? Similarly, what is the effect of sequenced learning hierarchies in acquiring concepts via computers?

Question 5: Games

We also need to know more about the effects of games on learners. How can they help students acquire computer literacy? Are drill games truly beneficial? Can students acquire abstract concepts via games? What about the comparative efficiency of learning via games and learning in other ways? Finally, what are the political risks inherent in using games for educational purposes?

We could ask many more questions about such variables as color, sound, time on task, attitude, and problem solving. An entirely new area of educational research has opened up and it's time that we started looking at these questions seriously.

II. Choosing Computers for Education

4. Some Basic Information About Computers

M. Tim Grady

THE COMPUTER'S USEFULNESS COMES FROM ITS CAPABILITY to accept, manipulate, and display data. In order to process the data, it has to store and execute programs.

Some typical types of computers are the mainframe, the minicomputer, the microcomputer, and the personal computer.

The **mainframe,** or large computer, is an ultra-high-speed processor that can support several users performing a variety of tasks all at the same time. The mainframe also supports large memory devices and an array of peripheral devices such as card readers, tape drives, and printers. Monitors and operating systems of the mainframe allow it to use more than one computer language.

The **minicomputer** differs from the mainframe in size, speed, and the number of tasks it can perform simultaneously. Usually it has a fairly sophisticated operating system and a large memory, and can work in several languages. Typically, the minicomputer is used in a time-sharing arrangement, which means that a number of terminals are connected to the same machine.

The **microcomputer** is slower, has less memory, and is generally considered to be a single-user machine. Its name comes from the fact that the processor is a microprocessor, usually a single chip. New advances in microprocessor technology are allowing for more memory and more users per machine, and are making the distinction between micros and minis less clear.

Personal computers are considered to be at the lower end of the microcomputer line. They are the simplest to use, but they can handle only one user and one task at a time. They also have limited language capability, so software designed for one make of machine may not work on a different brand.

A main characteristic of a computer is its **memory,** the ability to retain data and programming information. Memory devices have evolved over the years from tubes to transitors to integrated circuits or solid state memories.

The information stored in a computer system is usually referred to in terms of **bytes.** In general, a computer defines a character or a symbol as a series of ones and zeros. The position of place value of a one or a zero is called a **bit.** Bytes are made up of bits in a microcomputer memory.

It's common for microcomputer ads to refer to 16K bytes, 32K bytes, 48K bytes, and so on. This simply means that the computer's memory is capable of storing 16,000, 32,000, 48,000, or more characters. A single **character** is defined internally as eight bits, or one byte. In other words, a character is equivalent to a byte. The characters can be data, program steps, or a combination of both.

Many microcomputers are "eight bit" machines, which means they can process only eight bits of data, one at a time. They can, however, link two bytes together, which yields 16 different routes, or lines, to the memory, so the amount of memory is limited to the maximum number of combinations of ones and zeros in 16 positions—about 64K.

Newer microcomputers are using 16 bit microprocessors. The chief advantage of this system is that it can address far more memory locations. For years, large mainframes have been 24 and 32 bit machines.

Memory available for use by programmers is called **RAM,** or "random access memory." Memory that can be read but not erased is called **ROM,** or "read only memory." Most microcomputers contain a substantial amount of ROM in which permanent programs such as graphics, sound, and languages are stored. Any ROM present in a microcomputer reduces the amount of RAM available for programming. The key question a prospective buyer should ask is, "How much usable memory is available for programmer use?"

In order to store programs and data for future use, computers need external storage devices. Schools are generally interested in low cost, reliable storage devices. **Cassette tape** is the least expensive device, but it's very slow because its storage is "sequential"—the computer can't quickly skip from one place to another as it can with a disk.

Floppy disk drives provide the lowest cost random access storage for micros. They are relatively fast, but a single diskette is limited in the amount of storage it provides.

Winchester fixed disks are a new alternative to the floppy disk drive. They provide much more storage capability per unit than do floppy disks and are much faster in access time. Their disadvantages are that they require some form of large-scale back-up and that they're expensive. The cost of Winchester disks rules them out for nonadministrative applications in most school districts, but they may be used to store essential data bases such as student attendance files.

An important part of most computer installations is the **printer,** which is like a high speed typewriter and is used to print out anything the user wants to have on paper. A variety of printers are available at prices generally dependent on their speed of operation and print quality.

Dot matrix printers form characters one at a time. Their chief advantages are their low cost and their printing speed, which is usually from 90 to 200 characters per second.

"Daisy wheel printers," or "character printers," provide a correspondence quality output. In other words, the letters formed on this type of printer rival a good typewriter for quality. This printer is slow, however—25 to 60 characters per second—and its cost is higher than a dot matrix printer.

Mainframe computers usually employ very high speed line printers and/or laser printers. These machines are quite expensive and aren't ordinarily used with microcomputers.

A programmer communicates with a computer by using a special language. Most microcomputers speak BASIC, which means "Beginners All-purpose Symbolic Instruction Code." BASIC is relatively easy to use.

Computers really only understand combinations of ones and zeros, so the computer has to have another program that translates the user's statements into **machine language.** The translator is either an interpreter or a compiler. Most microcomputers use interpreters, which are easy to use but don't work as fast as compiler-based languages.

COBOL and FORTRAN are two other popular languages. Because they are compiler-based languages, they are more difficult to use, but they're a lot faster than BASIC.

PASCAL is a language that comes in different forms. In some cases it's a compiler language, and in others it's an operating system.

Because of BASIC's simplicity, most school programs use an interpreted BASIC language. However, the business world is heavily committed to compiler languages, so programming classes should provide experience with them.

An **assembly language** is somewhere between the higher level languages and machine language. It is highly symbolic and uses abbreviated codes. The advantages are efficiency of memory and speed

Programming classes should also provide some background in assembly languages.

The computer is here to stay. It will be used even more extensively in the years ahead than it is today. With careful planning and preparation, you can help your school make a smooth transition to the computer age.

5. Resources for Instructional Computing

Judith Edwards Allen

THE PHONE CALL IS A FAMILIAR ONE TO THOSE WHO OFFER ASSISTANCE to educators in computer use. It usually follows the initial call ("What computer should we buy?") by two to four weeks. Often the caller—a central office administrator, curriculum worker, teacher, or principal— is desperate or at least feeling out-of-sorts and misled. He or she has by now acquired a microcomputer and has discovered that locating tested, high quality instructional software is not a straightforward task! The voice on the other end of the line is plaintive, sometimes seeking a culprit. "WHERE is the software??? HOW do I find it? WHO knows if it's worth the money? WHY didn't anyone warn me about the software situation? WHEN will the software be as good and as easy to get as the hardware???"

Other calls, less desperate, come from those who are exploring software prior to acquiring hardware. The questions, however, are the same.

Fortunately, there are some answers. The software situation is not as grim as it was even a year ago and today the challenge to the curriculum decision maker is to somehow select the appropriate software (or "courseware") from the increasing variety of packages available from a wide range of sources.

One is tempted to begin with a free public lecture on the virtues of careful planning for computer use in education. We all know that software should be reviewed and selected before hardware decisions are made. Reality intrudes, however. Half of the nation's schools already have at least one microcomputer and many schools have an assortment: one PET, two Apples, three TRS-80s, and one something-else, for example. These computers have been acquired in very resourceful ways: kids sell cookies and wash cars to raise money; the PTA buys a micro for the school; the parents sponsor an "Apple Dance;" the 5th graders write letters as a language arts exercise asking businesses for donations; some year-end money becomes available; Title IV-C funds or gifted and talented funds are used; or a benevolent supporter donates a microcomputer to the school. The current fascination with microcomputers leaves educators scrambling to explore and demonstrate the potential of this exciting resource, often spurred by the arrival of an unsolicited microcomputer at the door.

At a few schools, the scramble is powered by anxiety as the new computer becomes an extension of the arcade. In the absence of a collection of high quality software or a plan for using the computer, games fill the void.

Whether a school or district is beginning the planning process, seeking software for one or an assortment of already-acquired microcomputers, or expanding a computer education program, there are a variety of excellent resources available, and new ones are constantly appearing.

The list of resources that follows is a representative sampling of information of particular interest to educators using (or contemplating the use of) microcomputers in elementary and secondary school settings. The following categories are used: Indexes/Bibliographies; Books; Journals, Periodicals, and Newsletters; Educational Courseware Reviews and Guides to Hardware Selection; On-line Information Services; Associations and User Groups; Centers and Clearinghouses; Computer Literacy; and Other Technologies.

Please remember that prices, telephone numbers, and other particulars are subject to change.

Indexes/Bibliographies

THE MICROCOMPUTER INDEX
2464 El Camino Real
Santa Clara, California 95051

This quarterly publication is a subject-indexed collection of abstracts from some 23 computing magazines. It is available online through Dialog Information Services, an information utility operated by Lockheed Corporation.

REFERENCE MANUAL FOR INSTRUCTIONAL USE OF
MICROCOMPUTERS
JEM Research
Discovery Park
University of Victoria
P.O. Box 1700
Victoria, British Columbia V8W 2Y2
Canada
This is a comprehensive reference manual with a wealth of descriptive information on over 1,000 educational courseware programs from elementary school to university levels. Programs are indexed and cross referenced according to subject and grade level. Over 200 courseware evaluations are included, along with a list of publishers and an annotated index of books, magazines, and journals on microcomputer technology and computer literacy. The courseware index and publisher list are also available on seven data disks for educators who own MicroLab's The Data Factory.

1983 CLASSROOM COMPUTER NEWS DIRECTORY OF
EDUCATIONAL COMPUTING RESOURCES
Classroom Computer News
341 Mt. Auburn St.
Watertown, Massachusetts 02172
This directory provides information on courseware, computers, associations, periodicals, local and regional consortia and groups involved in educational computing projects.

Books

PRACTICAL GUIDE TO COMPUTERS IN EDUCATION, by Peter Coburn and others. Reading, Massachusetts: Addison-Wesley Publishing Company, 1982. Written for teachers, administrators, and interested parents, the purpose of this book is to introduce the novice to computers in the general setting of schools. Descriptive vignettes accompany information on the working of computers, their potential applications, and suggestions about how to establish a computer resource in the school. It contains an excellent bibliography (annotated), resource listings, a glossary, and an index.

COMPUTER-ASSISTED INSTRUCTION USING BASIC, by John F. Huntington. Englewood Cliffs, New Jersey: Educational Technology Publications, 1979. This is a "starter" book for teachers or trainers who are novices at both instructional design and programming. The emphasis is on BASIC procedures for writing CAI programs.

MICROCOMPUTERS IN THE SCHOOLS, edited by James L. Thomas. Phoenix: The Onyx Press, 1981. A collection of articles written by experts and professionals, this book is divided into sections on selection, hardware and software development, curriculum applications and trends and issues. It contains a useful bibliography and appendices.

LEARNING ALTERNATIVES IN U.S. EDUCATION: WHERE STUDENTS AND COMPUTERS MEET, by Beverly Hunter and others. Englewood Cliffs, New Jersey: Educational Technology Publications, 1975. Somewhat dated, but nevertheless a helpful resource for decision makers.

MICROCOMPUTERS IN EDUCATION: A NONTECHNICAL GUIDE TO INSTRUCTIONAL AND SCHOOL MANAGEMENT APPROACHES, by Lee Marvin Joiner and others. Holmes Beach, Florida: Learning Publications, Inc., 1982. This is a very practical and accessible discussion of the state of the art in using microcomputers in school management. It also contains useful information on administrative applications.

MINDSTORMS: CHILDREN, COMPUTERS AND POWERFUL IDEAS, by Seymour Papert. New York: Basic Books, 1980. Written by the leader of the team that created LOGO, a computer language originally developed for children, this book presents a vision of what might be possible using computers as a learning resource.

"STUDY OF ISSUES RELATED TO IMPLEMENTATION OF COMPUTER TECHNOLOGY IN SCHOOLS," by Karen Scheingold and others. Final Report to NIE. Bank Street College of Education, July 1981. This report contains a series of case studies of school districts that have attempted to use computers in the classroom. Among the findings of this important study is that girls are not getting as much access to computers as boys because they are subtly and perhaps unintentionally being guided away from activities involving the computers.

THE COMPUTER IN THE SCHOOL: TUTOR, TOOL, TUTEE, edited by Robert P. Taylor. New York: Teachers College Press, 1980. This collection of essays is aimed at introducing the work of five pioneers in the use of computers in education: Alfred Bork, Thomas Dwyer, Arthur Luehrmann, Seymour Papert, and Patrick Suppes. The essays by Bork in particular are essential for anyone attempting to develop computer-assisted instruction. The book contains a useful bibliography and an index.

COMPUTER TECHNOLOGY IN CURRICULUM AND INSTRUCTION HANDBOOK, by the Washington Superintendent of Public Instruction. Olympia, Washington, 1982 (contact Sue Collins or Elden Egbers). A useful collection of resources and information for teachers, curriculum workers, or administrators. It is divided into six separate guides: (1) Introduction, (2) So You Want To Use Computers, (3) Design for Staff Development, (4) Courseware Evaluation, (5) Resources, and (6) Practitioners' Directory.

Journals, Periodicals, and Newsletters

ACCESS: MICROCOMPUTERS IN LIBRARIES. P.O. Box 764. Oakridge, OR 97463. Published quarterly. Subscription: $11.00 per year.

AEDS JOURNAL. 1201 Sixteenth Street, N.W., Washington, DC 20036. Published four times per year. Subscription: Included in $35.00 AEDS dues or $25.00 for non-AEDS members. This journal prints articles, research, evaluations, and other papers relating to the field of educational computing. It encourages articles pertaining to "administrative or instructional uses of computers."

AEDS MONITOR. 1201 Sixteenth Street, N.W., Washington, DC 20036. Published quarterly. Subscription: $15.00. This publication prints articles of popular and practical interest on educational computing.

ARITHMETIC TEACHER. National Council of Teachers of Mathematics, 1906 Association Drive, Reston, VA 22091. Published nine times annually. Subscription: $30.00. This math journal carries a regular column reviewing math software.

BYTE. 70 Main Street, Peterborough, NH 03458. Published twelve times per year. Subscription: $19.00. BYTE contains occasional articles on educational uses of computers and is a well-established, well-respected journal covering nearly every aspect of microcomputing.

CLASSROOM COMPUTER NEWS. Intentional Educations, Inc., 51 Spring Street, Watertown, MA 02171. Published bimonthly. Subscription: $16.00. This journal is targeted exclusively on the classroom uses of computers. It includes articles that are appropriate for teachers who are just beginning to use computers, as well as for more experienced teachers.

CLOAD MAGAZINE. This is not actually a magazine, but rather a cassette tape for a TRS-80 microcomputer with supporting documentation.

COMPUTE! The Journal for Progressive Computing. Box 5406, Greensboro, NC 27403. Published twelve times annually. Subscription: $20.00. This publication features articles of interest to users of micros based on the 6502 microprocessor. Apple, PET, and Atari are all 6502-based machines.

COMPUTER LITERACY NEWS. HumRRO, 300 N. Washington Street, Alexandria, VA 22314. This newsletter is distributed to persons requesting information from HumRRO. HumRRO (Human Resources Research Organization) is an independent nonprofit research group that conducts projects in computer literacy and other areas.

THE COMPUTING TEACHER. International Council for Computers in Education, Department of Computer and Information Science, University of Oregon, Eugene, OR 97403. Published nine times annually. Subscription: $14.50. One of the first journals for educators in the field, it contains articles and reviews, and includes MicroSIFT reviews. The journal emphasizes "teaching about computers, using computers, teacher education, and the impact of computers on curriculum."

COURSEWARE MAGAZINE. 4919 N. Millbrook, #222, Fresno, CA 93726. Published five times annually. Subscription: $65.00. This product consists of a cassette tape with educational programs. Tapes may be ordered for Apple, PET, or TRS-80 micros, and supporting documentation is included.

CREATIVE COMPUTING. Box 789-M, Morristown, NJ 07690. Published monthly. Subscription: $15.00. This publication includes articles for home users, educators, and kids.·

CUE NEWSLETTER. c/o Don McKell, Independence High School, 1776 Education Park Drive, San Jose, CA 95133. Published six times per year. Subscription: Newsletter included in $6.00 annual CUE (Computer Using Educators) dues. This newsletter is published by one of the largest user groups of computer educators in the nation.

CURRICULUM PRODUCT REVIEW: The Educators Guide to Instructional Materials. Pitman Learning, Inc., 530 University Avenue, Palo Alto, CA 94301. Published nine times annually.

EDUCATION TECHNOLOGY. 140 Sylvan Avenue, Englewood Cliffs, NJ 07632. Published monthly. Subscription: $49.00. This well-respected journal contains regular reviews of courseware as well as relevant articles on the use of computers in education.

ELECTRONIC EDUCATION. Electronic Communications, Inc., Suite 220, 1311 Executive Center Drive, Tallahassee, FL 32301. Published ten times annually. Subscription: $10.00.

EDUCATOR'S MICRODIGEST and SOFTWARE EXCHANGE. Educorp 21 Ltd., P.O. Box 162, Madison, WI 53791. Published monthly. Subscription: $63.00. This publication features computer software development for vocational educators.

ELECTRONIC LEARNING: The Magazine for Educators of the 80s. Scholastic, Inc., 902 Sylvan Avenue, Englewood Cliffs, NJ 07632. Published eight times annually. Subscription: $19.00.

INFOWORLD. 375 Cochituate Road, Box 880, Framingham, MA 01701. Published 51 times annually. Subscription: $25.00. In tabloid format, this publication is packed with new developments and trade news. It contains hardware and software reviews as well as other features.

INSTRUCTIONAL INNOVATOR. 1126 Sixteenth St., N.W., Washington, DC 20036. Published eight times per year. Included as part of AECT membership; $24.00 annually to nonmembers. This is the official publication of the Association for Educational Communications and Technology.

INTERFACE AGE. 16704 Marquardt Avenue, Cerritos, CA 90701. Published monthly. Subscription: $18.00. This journal features articles of interest to the business and home micro user.

JOURNAL OF COURSEWARE REVIEW. Apple Educational Foundation, 20525 Mariani, Cupertino, CA 95014. Published quarterly. Subscription: $5.95 per issue. Contains reviews of educational software for personal computers.

MACUL JOURNAL. Michigan Association for Computer Users in Learning, Wayne County ISD, 33500 Van Born Road, Wayne, MI 48184. Published two–three times annually. Subscription: Included with $5.00 MACUL membership dues. This journal includes an annual evaluation issue with extensive courseware reviews.

MATHEMATICS TEACHER. National Council of Teachers of Mathematics, 1906 Association Drive, Reston, VA 22091. Published nine times annually. Subscription: Included in $30.00 NCTM membership.

MEDIA & METHODS: The Magazine of the Teaching Technologies. 1511 Walnut Street, Philadelphia, PA 19102. Published nine times per year. Subscription: $24.00.

MICROCOMPUTERS IN EDUCATION. Queue, Inc., 5 Chapel Hill Drive, Fairfield, CT 06432. Published monthly. Subscription: $28.00. This newsletter contains reviews and information related to the instructional uses of computers.

MICROCOMPUTING (formerly Kilobaud Microcomputing). 80 Pine Street, Peterborough, NH 03458. Published monthly. Subscription: $25.00. This publication is mainly written for serious computer users, and features articles written by readers.

PERSONAL COMPUTING. 50 Essex Street, Rochelle Park, NJ 07662. Published monthly. Subscription: $18.00.

PIPELINE. Conduit, University of Iowa, Box 388, Iowa City, IA 52244. Published three times per year. Subscription: $15.00. This journal is principally targeted to higher education articles. Each issue includes descriptions of new courseware offerings.

RECREATIONAL COMPUTING, P.O. Box E, Menlo Park, CA 94025. Published bimonthly. Subscription: $12.00.

SCHOOL MICROWARE REVIEWS. Dresden Associates, P.O. Box 246, Dresden, ME 04342. Published biannually. Subscription: $20.00 per issue. This journal is devoted exclusively to courseware reviews and includes an index to reviews in other publications as well as a description of the evaluation process.

SMALL COMPUTERS IN LIBRARIES. Graduate Library School, University of Arizona, 1515 E. First Street, Tucson, AZ 85721. Published monthly. Subscription: $20.00.

SOFTALK. 11021 Magnolia Boulevard, North Hollywood, CA 91601. Published monthly. Subscription: complimentary trial subscription to Apple computer owners; $24.00 per year without sponsor, $18.00 with sponsor. This journal is aimed exclusively at owners of Apple computers.

SOFTWARE REVIEW. Microform Review, 520 Riverside Avenue, Westport, CT 06880. Published twice yearly. Subscription: $38.00.

T.H.E. JOURNAL. P.O. Box 992, Acton, MA 01720. Published six times per year. Subscription: Free to qualified educators.

TRS-80 MICROCOMPUTER NEWS. P.O. Box 2910, Fort Worth, TX 76113. Published monthly. Subscription: $12.00. Journal available free for six months for owners of Radio Shack TRS-80 computers.

Educational Courseware Reviews/Guides to Hardware Selection

Hardware Guides

Numerous "buyer's guides" exist; nearly every major computing magazine has published at least one. The articles below represent a sampling of what is available.

"COMPUTER BUYER'S GUIDE, PART 2." *Popular Computing* 1 (August 1982). A useful, up-to-date survey of available small computers, summarizing a variety of features. Part 1 of this buyer's guide dealt with business computers and appeared in previous issues.

CREATIVE COMPUTING 1 (September 1981). Entire issue is a 304-page buyer's guide to microcomputers and peripheral devices, video and electronic games, electronic learning aids, and consumer electronics. For $2.50, it is one of the best single resources available to the computer buyer.

"PERSONAL COMPUTERS, TAKE YOUR PICK," by Tom Fox in *Interface Age* 6 (April 1981): 46.

"HOW TO SELECT A PERSONAL COMPUTER," by David D. Thornburg in *Recreational Computing* 10 (July–August 1981): 8.

"PERSONAL COMPUTERS: PRODUCTS FOR EVERY NEED," *Personal Computing* 5 (May 1981): 45.

"ADDING A MICRO TO YOUR SCHOOL PICTURE," by K. Billings and S. Glass in *Electronic Learning* (January–February 1982): 35.

Courseware Reviews

AEDS MONITOR 20 (April, May, June 1982). Series of articles on evaluation of educational software, including sample materials and discussions of issues by several top practitioners and developers.

EPIE (Educational Products Information Exchange), an agency that regularly reviews and reports on educational products. Report on educational software that covers mostly math software, and is available from the following address: EPIE Report #98-99M, EPIE Institute, Box 620, Stony Brook, NY 11790. Price: $25.00.

"MICROCOMPUTER SOFTWARE FOR INSTRUCTIONAL USE: WHERE ARE THE CRITICAL REVIEWS?" by Ann Lathrop in *The Computing Teacher* 9 (February 1982): 22–26. Article analyzes existing journals, including those listed in the previous section, regarding the type and quality of courseware reviews appearing in them.

MICROSIFT. MicroSIFT stands for Microcomputer Software Information for Teachers, and is a project of the Computer Technology Program of the Northwest Regional Educational Laboratory. With the help of a 26-member user network, MicroSIFT coordinates the systematic evaluation of educational courseware aimed at elementary and secondary classrooms. Results of evaluations have been made available to several of the magazines and journals listed above, and are placed in ERIC. Evaluations are also disseminated through some state Departments of Education and regional educational agencies. Evaluations will also be available via the RICE database (see below). The Evaluator's Guide is available through ERIC or the International Consortium for Computers in Education (ICCE). For further information, contact the Computer Technology Program, Northwest Regional Educational Laboratory, 300 S.W. Sixth Avenue, Portland, OR 97204.

MINNESOTA EDUCATIONAL COMPUTING CONSORTIUM (MECC). Coordinates and provides computer programs and services to educators in Minnesota. One of the first such statewide efforts in the nation, MECC has published a Computer Courseware Review Form that is available without charge from MECC, Instructional Systems Development, 2520 Broadway Drive, St. Paul, MN 55113.

NATIONAL COUNCIL OF TEACHERS OF MATHEMATICS (NCTM). NCTM has published Guidelines for Evaluating Computerized Instructional Materials, providing information for educators about the locations, selection, and evaluation of computerized materials. The publication is available from NCTM, 1906 Association Drive, Reston, VA 22091. Price: $3.75 for 26-page set of guidelines that lists sources of information about commercial and noncommercial computerized instructional materials. Also contains an evaluation model and checklist.

SCHOOL MICROWARE: A DIRECTORY OF EDUCATIONAL SOFTWARE. Available on the ERIC system, describes over 500 programs and packages for Apple, PET, and TRS-80 users. It can also be ordered from Dresden Associates, P.O. Box 246, Dresden, ME 04342.

"EDUCATIONAL SOFTWARE FOR THE HOME," by Lee The in *Personal Computing* 6 (June 1982). Article that takes in-depth look at perspectives on educational software and quotes extensively from software developers. Contains helpful guidelines for evaluating educational software.

On-Line Information Services

RICE. Resources in Computer Education, a project of the Computer Technology Program at the Northwest Regional Educational Laboratory, is the nation's first comprehensive data base on microcomputer software for elementary and secondary education. The RICE database is made up of five files: Software Packages presents information on upwards of 2,000 courseware packages, including any available evaluations. The Producers file contains information on producers of courseware for both educational and administrative uses. The Computer Literacy file contains objectives and test items related to computer literacy; and the Project Register file lists information about projects in which the computer is used to enhance education. Finally, the Inventory file has information about where and how computers are being used in elementary and secondary schools. The first two files are now available to the public and the remaining three files will soon be publicly available.

RICE is available through Bibliographic Retrieval Services (BRS), an information utility. Schools wishing to use the RICE database will be able to do so with any microcomputer or terminal and a telephone. The agency must also join the School Practices Information Network (SPIN), a network of interested educators established by BRS. Further information may be obtained from BRS, 1200 Route 7, Latham, NY 12110, (518) 783-1161.

SPIN/SPIF. As mentioned above, SPIN stands for the School Practices Information Network; SPIF stands for the School Practices Information File, a resource file of validated programs, practices, and materials. SPIN/SPIF represents the first attempt to facilitate the sharing of educational practice information among educational agencies and institutions through the use of advanced telecommunications and computer technology.

Associations and User Groups

ASSOCIATION FOR COMPUTING MACHINERY (ACM)
1133 Avenue of the Americas
New York, NY 10036
(212) 265-6300

Publications: Communications, Computing Reviews, ACM Guide to Computer Science and Computer Applications Literature, ACM SIG-CUE Bulletin. An organization of primarily higher education computer scientists, with a subgroup (ACM SIGCUE) for those interested in educational applications.

ASSOCIATION FOR EDUCATIONAL COMMUNICATION AND TECH-NOLOGY (AECT)
1126 Sixteenth Street, N.W.
Washington, DC 20036
(202) 833-4180

Publications: Educational Communication and Technology Journal, Journal of Instructional Development, Instructional Innovator. An organization of people involved with "media" of all kinds, now including computers and telecommunications.

ASSOCIATION FOR EDUCATIONAL DATA SYSTEMS (AEDS)
1201 Sixteenth Street, N.W.
Washington, DC 20036
(202) 833-4100

Publications: AEDS Bulletin, AEDS Monitor, AEDS Journal, AEDS Handbook. An organization of educators involved in educational computing, primarily at the K–12 level. Focus of instructional applications and administrative systems.

ASSOCIATION FOR THE DEVELOPMENT OF COMPUTER-BASED INSTRUCTIONAL SYSTEMS (ADCIS)
Computer Center
Western Washington State University
Bellingham, WA 98225
(206) 676-2860

Publications: The Journal of Computer-Based Instruction, ADCIS Newsletter. An organization of primarily higher education scientists involved in R&D related to design and development of computer software for instruction.

COMPUTER-USING EDUCATORS (CUE)
c/o Don McKell
Independence High School
1775 Educational Park Drive
San Jose, CA 95113

Organizes conferences, publishes a bimonthly newsletter, is a joint sponsor of Softswap (see "clearinghouses" below). Membership is available from the address above.

INTERNATIONAL COUNCIL FOR COMPUTERS IN EDUCATION (ICCE)
Department of Computer and Information Science
University of Oregon
Eugene, OR 97403
(503) 686-4414

Publications: The Computing Teacher; ICCE also makes available several other important publications for educators interested in microcomputing, including the Evaluator's Guide (developed by MicroSIFT), Introduction to Computers in Education for Elementary and Middle School Teachers, and School Administrator's Introduction to Instructional Use of Computers.

NATIONAL COUNCIL OF TEACHERS OF MATHEMATICS (NCTM)
1906 Association Drive
Reston, VA 22091
(703) 620-9840

Publications: Arithmetic Teacher, Mathematics Teacher, Guidelines for Evaluating Computerized Instructional Materials. Users groups based on particular machines (for example, Apple, PET, TRS-80, Atari, and so on) also exist in many locales. Consult with other computer users or with your supplier for up-to-date information on what is available in your area.

Centers, Clearinghouses, and Support Agencies

CONDUIT
P.O. Box 388
Iowa City, IA 52244
(319) 355-5789

While the primary focus of activities is on courseware for higher education, many of the programs Conduit reviews and distributes are appropriate for advanced high school classes. Conduit has published an Author's Guide, a model for establishing guidelines in developing and evaluating software.

MICROCOMPUTER CENTER
San Mateo County Office of Education
333 Main Street
Redwood City, CA 94063
(415) 363-5472
(see Softswap below)

MICROSIFT
Computer Technology Program
Northwest Regional Educational Laboratory
300 S.W. Sixth Avenue
Portland, OR 97204
(503) 248-6800
(see MicroSIFT under "Educational Courseware Reviews" above)

MINNESOTA EDUCATIONAL COMPUTING CONSORTIUM (MECC)
2520 Broadway Drive
St. Paul, MN 55113
(612) 376-1101
(see MECC under "Educational Courseware Reviews" above)

OFFICE OF TECHNOLOGY ASSESSMENT
U.S. Congress
Washington, DC 20510
(202) 224-3817

This federal agency is soon to release a comprehensive report entitled
Information Technology and its Impacts on American Education that
will discuss not only computer literacy, but also a full range of issues
related to varied information technologies and their patterns of use.

PROJECT BEST
1126 16th Street, N.W.
Washington, DC 20036
(202) 466-3361

This project provides a clearinghouse to help educators learn about
how information technology is being used around the nation.

SOFTSWAP
San Mateo County Office of Education
333 Main Street
Redwood City, CA 94063
(415) 363-5472

Softswap may copy any or all of these programs without charge, if they supply blank diskettes.

TECHNICAL EDUCATION RESEARCH CENTERS (TERC)
Computer Resource Center
8 Eliot Street
Cambridge, MA 02138
(617) 547-3890

Computer Literacy

Curriculum

"COMPUTERONICS." "Computeronics" is a nationally validated model for teaching computer literacy. Originally developed in Florida for gifted students, it was field tested with 6th and 7th graders. Subsequent users have included urban schools, middle and junior high schools, and gifted as well as undesignated students. Training is available for teachers desiring to use "Computeronics," and is recommended. "Computeronics" is designed for use with any kind of hardware, and the recommended ratio of computers to students is 1 to 8. For further information, contact: Diane Johnson, Gifted Child Project, Leon County School Board, 2757 West Pensacola, Tallahassee, FL 32304.

MY STUDENTS USE COMPUTERS. "My Students Use Computers" is an NSF-funded effort involving HumRRO and the Montgomery County, Maryland, public schools. The aim of the project is to help staff and teachers infuse computer-related objectives and activities into science, social studies, and math curricula for grades K–8. The curriculum is designed to support "universal computer literacy," which is defined as "skills and knowledge needed by all citizens to survive and thrive in a society that is dependent on technology for handling information and solving complex problems." A User's Guide describing this process for infusing computer literacy was scheduled for completion in 1,982. For further information, contact Beverly Hunter, HumRRO, 300 North Washington Street, Alexandria, VA 22314.

Horn, Carin E., and James L. Poirot. COMPUTER LITERACY: PROBLEM-SOLVING WITH COMPUTERS. Austin, TX: Sterling Swift Publishing Co., 1981, 304 pp. $13.95 + instructional manual $7.95 (free on adoption). This book is appropriate for use with junior high to adult age groups. It is intended for audiences needing introductory material on computers. The text is supported with ample visual material.

Graham, Neill. THE MIND TOOL: Computers and Their Impact on Society. 2nd ed. St. Paul: West Publishing Co., 1980, 398 pp. This book is written at the high school level and provides a comprehensive introduction to computers, their operation, and their roles in society. It also contains an introduction to BASIC. Exercises and an index are also included.

Rice, Jean, and Sandy O'Connor. COMPUTERS ARE FUN. Minneapolis: T. S. Denison and Company, Inc., 1981, 62 pp. $3.95 + Teacher's Guide and Activity Book. 92 pp. $12.00. These materials are designed to introduce 4–9 year olds to beginning computer concepts. The Teacher's Guide contains unit outlines, chapter aids, and masters for duplicating.

Rice, Jean. MY FRIEND THE COMPUTER. Minneapolis: T. S. Denison and Company, Inc., 1981 (revised). 96 pp. $4.95 + Teacher's Guide and Activity Book. 61 pp. + 42 duplicating masters. $15.00. These materials are intended for use with grades 4–7. The content focuses on an introduction to computers and their uses. The Teacher's Guide contains pre- and post-tests with answer keys and duplicating masters.

Rogers, Jean B. AN INTRODUCTION TO COMPUTERS AND COMPUTING. Eugene, OR: International Council for Computer Education, 1981. 48 pp. $2.50. This booklet provides an outline and materials for a course in computer science at the secondary school level.

COMPUTER DISCOVERY. SRA Publishers, Palo Alto, CA. This is a computer literacy course for grades 5–12. Students interact with a microcomputer and follow test exercises in computer history, analysis and programming, hardware and software concepts, and the social and economic impacts of the computer.

Computer Education Objectives and Test Items

COURSE GOALS IN COMPUTER EDUCATION K–12. Portland, OR: Commercial Educational Distributing Services, 1979. This is a comprehensive set of goals that may be used in planning and evaluating a wide range of computer education curricula.

"CUPERTINO SCHOOL DISTRICT DEVELOPS COMPUTER LIT-
ERACY CURRICULUM," The Computing Teacher 9 (Sept. 1981): 27–
34. This article contains information about the curriculum in computer
literacy developed in Cupertino. Goals and objectives are listed.
Further information about the curriculum is available from Cupertone
Union School District, 10301 Vista Drive, Cupertino, CA 95014.

"DEVELOPING COMPUTER LITERACY IN K–12 EDUCATION,"
The Computing Teacher 9 (Nov. 1981): 43–48. This article presents the
results of the efforts of a group of teachers, supervisors, and administrators who met to develop a coordinated approach to teaching computer
literacy. Objectives are listed in the article; further information is
available from the Board of Cooperative Educational Services, Third
Supervisory District, Suffolk County, NY.

OBJECTIVES AND TEST ITEMS FOR EDUCATIONAL COMPUT-
ING. This is a set of student objectives for computer literacy and
computer science, with three test items for each objective, prepared by
the Northwest Regional Educational Laboratory for the Department of
Defense Dependents Schools. Objectives are available from Dennis
Bybee, Department of Defense, Office of Dependents Schools, 2461
Eisenhower Avenue, Room 172, Alexandria, VA 22331. The test item
bank is at NWREL, and is available in the form of tests.

Other Technologies

Condon, Joyce J. "EDUCATION CAN WIN BIG IN CABLE TV,"
Instructional Innovator 27 (May 1982). 18ff.

Sigel, Efrem, Ed. VIDEOTEXT: The Coming Revolution in Home/
Office Information Retrieval. White Plains, NY: Knowledge Industry
Publications, Inc., 1980.

Tydeman, Jhon, "VIDEOTEX." Media and Methods 18 (May–Jun
1982). 52ff.

Wood, R. Kent, and Wooley, Robert D., "AN OVERVIEW OF
VIDEODISC TECHNOLOGY and Some Potential Applications in the
Library, Information and Instructional Sciences." Syracuse University
Printing Services, 125 College Place, Syracuse, NY 13210. Order IR-50.
37 pp. $7.00.

6. Help!! What Computer Should I Buy???

Ludwig Braun

THE PLEA IN THE TITLE OF THIS CHAPTER HAS BEEN MADE to me hundreds of times in the past three years by educators and administrators all over the United States. These people are bewildered by the technology and its capabilities, by the large number of companies marketing microcomputers, by the rapid rate of new developments in microcomputer technology, and by the wide range of models and peripherals available.

Computer companies perceive the education market as lucrative. As a result, they direct slick TV ads and very persuasive salespeople at educators.

Faced with pressures of staff, students, parents, and school boards to get their schools into computing, educators seek advice from any quarter about which machines to buy. Salespeople usually are more interested in making a sale than they are in meeting the needs of their customers. Because many educators have no competent, objective person to give them the help they need, they turn to the salespeople for advice and sometimes buy computers that do not meet their needs. The result is frustration, disappointment, and, frequently, disenchantment with the entire concept of computers in education.

Properly chosen and properly used, computers can make important contributions to the learning environments of children. The purpose of this chapter is to help educators make good decisions about equipment for their school systems.

Purchasing computer hardware and software may be compared to purchasing automobiles. On our roads we see a wide range of automobile models with different-size interiors, different engine power, front-

or rear-wheel drive, manual or automatic transmissions, two or four doors, and so on. Some people buy Fords, some Chevrolets, and some Toyotas. The automobile owner uses a variety of criteria—some objective and some subjective—to make a decision about the automobile to buy. The diversity of cars on the road indicates that there is no single automobile that is the best—just as there is no single microcomputer that is the best in every educational situation. I will not tell the reader which computer to buy or which to avoid. I *will* suggest a set of criteria that is useful as a guide in making the decision and a rational way of applying these criteria to all computers under consideration.

A Few Basic Guidelines

I consider the following guidelines basic to the decision-making process and more important than the size of the memory, the language features, and other criteria that people usually apply.

a. *Get the most entry ports that your budget permits.* This is so obvious that it shouldn't need to be said; however, there are educators who buy a single computer costing many thousands of dollars rather than five, or even ten, simpler computers for the same total. Whatever the capability of the expensive machine, the educator has the fundamental responsibility to maximize the educational impact of every dollar he or she spends. The basic question here is, Does the powerful, but expensive, computer produce more educational "bang" than a group of simpler, but less costly, computers?

Primarily for this reason, the Compucolor, the micro PLATO, and the Terak computers will not be considered here, even though they are excellent computers with capabilities not available on the computers that will be considered in detail.

b. *Do not choose a particular computer unless there is a body of users of that computer in your region.* Most educators do not have a great deal of expertise concerning computer hardware or software. There is great value in joining a community of users. Such communities frequently form clubs for exchange of programs, ideas for application, and other experiences—good and bad. In a group it is likely that you will find someone else who has had (and solved) your problem— no matter what. If you are the only user of the XYZ computer in your region, you will be dependent on the manufacturers for help; and that has not proved to be a good source of help in at least some cases. For this reason we will consider in detail only the Apple, Commodore PET, and TRS-80 computers even though Atari, Heath, Ohio Scientific, Texas Instruments, and other companies make fine computers.

c. *Buy from a local dealer.* There are some computer dealers who advertise nationally and who offer computers at prices that sometimes are somewhat better than those of local dealers. Local dealers, however, provide local service and local maintenance and frequently will loan you a computer while yours is being repaired.

Educational institutions frequently are required to purchase from the low bidder. This may be a mistake when maintenance and machine availability are factored into the decision process. Sending a computer out of town for repair usually takes a month because of shipping delays. Such a hiatus will make the teacher and students unhappy and may jeopardize the computer program in the school.

d. *Buy peripherals with care.* There are many peripherals available for microcomputers. There are printers, disc drives, music generators, analog-to-digital converters, and light pens, to name just a few. Each peripheral you buy enhances the capability of the computer to which it is attached, but it also takes away money from the purchase of computers (cf. item *a*).

Probably the most valuable peripheral is a printer. There are times when hard copy is valuable for the student (for instance, to provide a listing in a programming course). Further, sending children home with a printout of what they did on the computer will convince many parents to support computers in their schools.

A disc drive is also useful because program loading is much faster (seconds compared to minutes) and more reliable.

It is possible to use a single printer and a single disc drive for ten or even twenty computers by cabling all the machines together and ensuring that only one student at a time accesses the printer or disc drive.

Other peripherals may be useful in special circumstances (such as music generators for music instruction and experimentation), but they should be purchased with item *a* in mind.

One final caveat for the educator: *don't wait for computer developments (price reductions or hardware improvements) to settle down.* If you "wait till next year," you will wait forever. The three best microcomputers for classroom applications are the Apple, the PET, and the TRS-80, all of which were introduced in 1977!

A Basis for Decision Making

In 1979, I proposed an approach for comparing computers that permits each educator to factor into the decision-making process the uniqueness of his or her environment and individual assessments of

Figure 1
Capability Vector for Several Personal Computers

Capability	Apple II (Note 1)	PET 4001-16N	PET 4001-16N Plus Graphics (Note 2)	TRS-80 Model III
1. Cost (note 3)	$1560	$759	$1209	$959
2. Portable	moderately (3 modules)	very (single unit and cassette)	very (single unit and cassette)	very (single unit and cassette)
	27 pounds	37 pounds	37 pounds	25 pounds
3. Memory				
a. ROM	12K	14K	14K	14K
b. RAM	16K	16K	16K	16K
c. Expandable to	48K RAM/24K ROM	32K RAM/26K ROM	32K RAM/26K ROM	48K RAM/14K ROM
4. Cassette reliability	moderate	high	high	moderate
5. Execution time of computation (note 4)	4.0 sec	4.5 sec	4.5 sec	7.4 sec
6. Program loading speed	730 bits/sec	410 bits/sec (note 5)	410 bits/sec (note 5)	500 or 1500 bits/sec (note 6)
7. Composite video or rf signal	composite video (note 7)	neither (note 8)	neither (note 8)	not available
8. Editing capability	moderately powerful	very powerful	very powerful	moderately powerful
9. Graphics resolution	280 × 190 (note 9)	160 × 100 (note 10)	320 × 200	48 × 128 rectangular blocks
10. Screen size (characters × lines)	40 × 24	40 × 25	40 × 25	64 × 16 or 32 × 16
11. Colors available	15 (low-resolution mode)	black and white only	black and white only	black and white only
12. User-definable graphics characters	yes	no	no	no
13. Keyboard				
a. Layout	good	excellent	excellent	good
b. Size	full size	full size	full size	full size
c. Number of keys	52	73	73	65

Notes for Figure 1

1. Apple II Plus with 16K RAM, 9-inch black-and-white monitor, and audio cassette recorder.

2. This configuration is the PET 4001-16N plus the MTU Visible Memory Module graphics package, which adds $450 to the system cost. It adds vector graphic capability to the PET's character-oriented graphics.

3. These costs are the net costs to educators in spring 1981. The PET cost reflects the three-for-two sale in force at Commodore; the Apple price includes a 5% educational discount; and the TRS-80 price includes an educational discount of 10%. Depending on quantities and the specific dealer, better prices may be possible.

4. Execution time is time to execute the program:

```
10 X = 0
20 FOR I = 1 TO 1000
30 X = X + 1
40 NEXT I
50 PRINT X
```

5. The effective loading speed is 410 bits/sec rather than the published value of 810 because of redundancy and error checking.

6. The loading speed is user selectable at either 500 or 1500 bits/sec.

7. rf modulator available for $30.

8. Plug-in unit with video output available for $38.

9. The Apple II has a high-resolution mode (280×192) with 6 colors or a low-resolution mode (40×48 blocks) with 15 colors.

10. The resolution of the PET is difficult to specify. The screen has 1000 screen positions (40 characters per line $\times$ 25 lines). Each character is defined by an 8×8 dot matrix, so that the potential resolution is 64,000 dots. Because only 128 graphic characters have been defined, the resolution was chosen as a compromise between 1000 and 64,000 on the basis that the average number of dots per character is 16.

11. Frequently a teacher will want to display the computer output on a large screen so that a group of students may see the computer screen simultaneously. This may be accomplished in two ways: *(a)* by using a video monitor or *(b)* by using a TV set. In the former case, a video signal (called a *composite video signal*) is required; whereas in the latter case, a signal (called an *rf signal*) from the computer must be connected to the antenna terminals of a TV set.

the extent to which each computer under consideration meets the educator's goals. The approach involves a three-step procedure.

1. *Identification of a set of capabilities of importance to the individual.* Figure 1 on pages 46–47 includes 13 capabilities that I consider to be important in my environment. A teacher who is interested in music instruction may wish to add music-generation capability to this figure. Others may not be interested in connecting external video monitors to the computer and may want to drop item 7 from the list. Any capabilities may be added to or subtracted from this figure to suit the individual situation.

2. *Assignment of an importance value to each of the capabilities in Figure 1.* The importance of a specific capability may be chosen (arbitrarily) to range from 0 to 100, with 100 considered to be very important and 0 considered to be unimportant. My assignments of importance are shown in Figure 2. I chose the set of importance values so that they total 100.

Figure 2
Importance Vector for Capabilities of Figure 1

Capability	Importance Value
1. Cost.............................	25
2. Portability..........................	10
3. Memory............................	0
4. Cassette reliability	5
5. Execution time	5
6. Program loading speed	10
7. Composite video or rf signal	10
8. Editing capability	10
9. Graphics resolution..................	15
10. Screen size	5
11. Colors available.....................	0
12. User-definable graphics..............	0
13. Keyboard	5
Total	100

3. *Assignment of a quality value to each of the capabilities in Figure 1 for each of the computers under consideration.* My assignments of quality for the Apple II, the Commodore PET, and the Radio Shack TRS-80 Model III are shown in Figure 3. In this figure there are two columns for the Commodore PET—one for the basic computer and

Figure 3
Quality Vectors for Computers of Figure 1

Capability	Apple II	PET 4001-16N	PET 4001-16N Plus Graphics	TRS-80 Model III
1. Cost	4.9	10	6.3	7.9
2. Portability	6	8	8	8
3. Memory	9.3	10	10	10
4. Cassette reliability	6	10	10	6
5. Execution time	10	8.9	8.9	5.4
6. Program loading speed	4.9	2.7	2.7	10
7. Composite video or rf signal	10	7	7	0
8. Editing capability	5	10	10	5
9. Graphics resolution	8.4	2.5	10	1
10. Screen size	9.4	9.8	9.8	10
11. Colors available	10	0	0	0
12. User-definable graphics	10	0	0	0
13. Keyboard	7	10	10	8.9

one for the computer with vector graphics capability. Each quality value is in the range of 0–10, with 10 being the highest value.

The set of importance values assigned in item 2 (Figure 3) may be represented by a vector with elements $I(n)$, and the set of quality values assigned in item 3 may be represented by a vector with elements $Q(n)$. The worth of a specific computer is the sum of products of the elements $I(n)$ and $Q(n)$. Mathematically,

$$\text{Worth} = \sum_{n-1}^{M} I(n) \times Q(n),$$

where M is the number of capabilities included in Figure 1.

It is of the utmost importance for the reader to be aware that the specific capabilities that are included in Figure 1 and the importance of quality values assigned in Figures 2 and 3 *were selected by me to fit my situation and my subjective interpretation of that situation.* Each person who uses this approach must choose a set of capabilities and sets of importance and quality values that correspond to his or her unique situation.

In Figure 2, for example, I gave the most weight to the importance of computer cost (in line with guideline *a*, mentioned earlier) and next most importance to graphics resolution, because mathematics teachers need high resolution to permit drawing of geometric figures and graphs of functions. I am not convinced of the value of color in most learning situations and assigned zero importance to it in Figure 2. The other values in Figure 2 were chosen on similar judgmental bases.

Some explanation of the quality values in Figure 3 is in order so that the reader can understand the approach. These values were chosen for the following reasons (in the order in which they appear in Figure 3).

1. *Cost.*

$$Q = \frac{\text{lowest cost}}{\text{cost}} \times 10.$$

2. *Portability.* The value here is based on the concept that more pieces mean less portability.

3. *Memory.*

$$Q = \frac{\text{memory}}{\text{largest memory}} \times 10.$$

4. *Cassette reliability.* The Apple and TRS-80 computers are standard audio cassette recorders and, depending on settings of volume and tone controls, can be unreliable—whereas in the PET a special cassette recorder is used without such controls and is more reliable.

5. *Execution time.*

$$Q = \frac{\text{fastest time}}{\text{time}} \times 10.$$

6. *Program loading speed.*

$$Q = \frac{\text{rate}}{\text{highest rate}} \times 10.$$

7. *Composite video or rf.* Apple has built-in composite video, the PET has a port to which an inexpensive adapter can be attached, and the TRS-80 has no capability for such a signal unless the user makes internal modifications.

8. *Editing capability.* The PET has excellent, easy-to-use screen-editing capability, which makes it simple to correct errors in program statements; the Apple has screen editing, but it is somewhat difficult to use; the TRS-80 has no line-editing capability, except by retyping a line.

9. *Graphics resolution.*

$$Q = \frac{\text{pixels}}{\text{largest number of pixels}} \times 10.$$

A pixel is a picture element. The PET with graphics, for example, has
320 × 200 = 64,000 pixels.

10. *Screen size.*

$$Q = \frac{\text{number of screen characters}}{\text{largest number of screen characters}} \times 10.$$

11. *Colors available.* Only the Apple has color capability.

12. *User-definable graphs.* Only the Apple has user-definable
graphic characters.

13. *Keyboard.*

$$Q = \frac{\text{number of keys}}{\text{largest number of keys}} \times 10.$$

If we use the worth equation with the importance and quality vectors of
Figures 2 and 3, the computers that we have considered are ranked as
follows:

Computer	Worth
PET with graphics board	778
PET without graphics board	758
Apple II	669.5
TRS-80 Model III	594

If one accepts the values chosen in Figures 2 and 3, the choice is
clear—almost. The PET with graphics and the PET without graphics
have worths that are almost identical. The essential differences between the two are in price and graphics resolution. To choose between
the two requires changing emphasis on these two capabilities.

It is my hope that the approach proposed in this article will help
educators to make the difficult decisions wisely and to avoid the traps
inherent in sales promotions.

The hardware decision already is difficult. As we learn more about
the Commodore VIC color computer for $300, the Radio Shack color

computer for $400, and the Sinclair ZX80 for $200, the decision will be even more difficult; but just think—a decade ago educators who used computers had almost no decisions to make, except whether to buy yellow or white paper for their teletypewriters. We are much luckier than they were. Our choices are exciting ones!

Bibliography

Braun, Ludwig. "How Do I Choose a Personal Computer?" *AEDS Journal* 13 (Fall 1979): 81–87.

Author's Note:
An Update

It is important that the reader understand that the preceding text was originally written in the spring of 1981. Since then, of course, computer technology has changed rapidly, as have the uses of various computers and their costs.

Even more significant is the fact that computers exist now which weren't even announced back in 1981 (such as the Sinclair/Timex ZX81 and the Commodore-64), and computers that weren't serious contenders at that time have begun to play an important role in educational computing (such as the Atari 400/800 machines). Had I been given the opportunity to revise this chapter before its publication here, these new machines would play a more prominent role in Figure 1 than would the Apple, PET, and Radio Shack machines listed there now.

The inadequacies of the data in Figure 1 are, however, unimportant since the thrust of this chapter is to present an *approach* to arriving at a decision rather than to make a recommendation of a specific machine.

After this chapter was published as an article in *The Mathematics Teacher* in November 1981, I received a number of comments from readers regarding (1) my lack of objectivity, (2) editing on the TRS-80, and (3) my selection criteria. Each of these matters merits attention.

1. Regarding my lack of objectivity. If you have ever discussed politics, religion, or what automobile to buy, you are aware that no one can approach such subjects with complete objectivity. And so it is with computers. Even at the outset I knew my conclusions would be biased by personal experiences and perceptions. And that is why I stated twice that readers should not consider my comments as a set of recommendations, but rather as a suggested approach to quantifying their own subjective reactions. Thus I must repeat: my choice of characteristics and my assignment of values for several machines were my own subjective choices and should not be considered as gospel.

I am constantly amazed that experts in this field, all presented with the same set of facts, come to radically different conclusions about which machine is the best! Unfortunately, no one can tell anyone else which computer is "best," just as no one can tell anyone else which car to buy or whom to marry.

2. Regarding editing on the Radio Shack computer. Although I stated in 1981 that the TRS-80 had only moderately powerful editing capabilities, I have since found that its editing capabilities are very powerful. Unfortunately, I based my comments on information I received from Radio Shack representatives, assuming, of course, that they were familiar with the capabilities of their machine. Apparently they didn't know the computer any better than I did.

3. Regarding my basic selection criteria. Clearly, each of us will choose a different set of criteria because we all have different needs, even though some of those needs and criteria may overlap.

The most serious criticism I received was about the fundamental process of first deciding what you want the computer to do and then choosing the computer best suited to do the job—including the selection of appropriate software. I would agree with this approach were I convinced that we really know how to use computers. While we know a fair amount by now, there are still many ways of using computers in learning that are only emerging and still other ways we haven't yet discovered.

Two years ago, for example, very few people considered the importance of word processing in teaching writing skills. Now many are exploring that approach. Two years ago, LOGO was a language that many thought might be important "someday." Now, with its availability on many micros, LOGO is used by elementary school children (and adults) everywhere. The Atari and Commodore 64 have very good musical capabilities and should become important in developing children's understanding of music. Yet this is still a largely undiscovered capability. Voice generation and recognition are also still primitive, but are improving every year. When they are well-developed, we may find that young children will be able to interact with computers in far more meaningful ways than are now possible, that we will be able to help people learn to speak properly, and that the physically handicapped will be able to accomplish things that are now beyond our imaginations.

We cannot restrict our choice of computers solely to those with applications we are currently aware of. We must pick the very best machines we can find, consistent with the need to provide significant computer access to as many children as our budgets can afford. If we base our choice merely on word processing, or graphics, or music, or programming language, or any other criterion of which we are presently aware, we will surely be sorry—because tomorrow a new mode of learning will emerge or a new computer capability (hardware or software) will be developed. We must approach these possibilities with an open mind and with the best computer capability we can get our hands on.

Editor's Note:
Shouldn't I Wait to Buy?

EACH MONTH COMPUTER RELATED MAGAZINES TELL OF NEW COMPUTERS. Each is reputed to be better than earlier models. Most are certainly cheaper. How can we know what to buy? Won't the price be reduced? The answer is probably, but slowly. The wise purchaser must be knowledgeable about the salient characteristics of the different genre.

In 1982–83, the current microcomputer offerings are roughly separated into five categories: (1) low-end personal computers and game machines, (2) personal computers, (3) small business versions of personal computers, (4) small CP/M based machines, and (5) desktop computers for small businesses. We need to place any computer we consider purchasing into one of these categories in order to make comparisons within that genre. Each category contains a range of models offered by different manufacturers. These models differ in their options and features much as automobiles differ. Within limits, individual purchasers should be influenced by the options that appeal to them.

The first category, low-end personal computers with game cartridges, are exemplified by the TI-99/4A, VIC-20, ATARI-400, TRS-80 colour computer, TIMEX 1000, and others. They are characterized by relatively low price, color graphics, sound, limited memory, and use of ROM cartridges for games and language expansion. A purchaser in this category will be swayed by price and styling. Schools can use these computers very effectively for CAI in the lower to intermediate elementary grades.

The second category, personal computers, is what all the fuss is about. The family sedan of microcomputers is exemplified by the TRS-80 I and II, PET, ATARI 800, APPLE II, Commodore 64, Franklin 1000 and others. Much like Fords and Chevys, the different models have developed great brand loyalties that will still be with us at the antique computer shows of the 90s. These machines are characterized by low resolution graphics, limited sound capabilities, a single old-fashioned processor, limited memory, and disk storage. Each model has strengths and weaknesses. The development of educational CAI software has focused on these computers. They are the best known type of micro among the educational community. Prices are competitive depending on options and styling. Educators will have trouble deciding on the "right" one; there is no right one. Hence, we try to make a deal for the model which appers to meet our needs most closely. Curriculum and instruction planners have made these computers the work horse of CAI in grades K–12.

The third category, enhanced versions of personal computers, generally have more sophisticated operating systems than their little brothers. They employ more memory, larger disk storage, and some have multiple processors. Examples of these machines are the TRS-80 Model 16, the Apple III, and Super Pet. Schools are generally using these computers in their high school computer classes and for limited administrative functions throughout the district.

The fourth category, CP/M-based small computers, is where it's at for small business systems. CP/M stands for Central Program for Microcomputers.* Since the late 70s these types of computers have been working in business, accounting, management, and related functions. They are exemplified by: XEROX- 820, MONROE, NEC PC8001, Superbrain, ALTOS, Vector Graphics, Burrough B-20, Univac's smallest, HP 125, and others. Priced at twice the value of personal computers, these machines have found limited use in CAI or CMI applications. Schools find them most attractive in administrative applications such as attendance, scheduling, staff development management, special education data management, and so forth.

---

*CP/M is a trademark of Digital Research, Inc.

The state of the art in microcomputers is exemplified by the last category, desktop computers, such as the IBM-PC, VICTOR 9000, Televideo, ALTOS 16 bit, HP-86, and others. The machines are characterized by higher speed, 16 bit and or multiple processors, larger amounts of memory, multiuser capability, larger disk storage, excellent business software, and $7 to $10 thousand price tags. Schools should only consider these computers for the high school classes and administrative support functions.

Choices seem at first to be vast and complicated. Actually, one can readily narrow the choice to one or two categories quite easily, depending on the application to be automated. Within any one category, the choices are further restricted by the availability of software for one's particular needs, service availability, and, of course, personal opinion on body style, color, and popularity.

Hardware technology is fast pushing forward. We can reasonably expect significant gains in the next few years. Already small microcomputers such as the Commodore 64 and APPLE II offer optional processors to enhance the flexibility and capability to their computers. Memory chip technology has significantly reduced the cost and physical space required to offer added memory. We can expect even more gains.

Networking has become popular in schools. It provides a means of having a larger number of keyboards and still have the advantages of disk storages. New technology in this area will allow us to network without the use of cumbersome cables. Fewer copies of software will be needed and management of the hardware/software inventory will be better.

Disk storage is still awkward. Flexible diskettes are too fragile and don't hold enough information. Winchester technology now offers greater capability. We can look forward to tremendous advances in data storage via very dense, environmentally robust and small "disks" that require no motors or heavy power supplies. Schools will be able to easily move computers around to meet their needs instead of forcing the students to come together in a lab or learning center.

Video display technology is improving. Flat screen displays are already offered by EPSON and Sinclair. The new advances in data storage and video display capability are going to have tremendous impact on schools by 1986.

As we plan for our schools, we need to try to meet our current needs. We also need to develop a ten-year plan for the future. We should try to read and stay up with technological advances. More importantly, we should work to incorporate these changes into our long-range plans.

7. Software Evaluation Criteria

M. Tim Grady

TEACHERS ARE BEING ASKED TO EVALUATE MICROCOMPUTER instructional software. The following are suggested guidelines for teachers and curriculum staff to use as they work in this area.

Two general parts are present in the evaluation. The first is simply the demographics of the intended use of the programs. The second is the performance criteria or "quality" aspect of the software.

The demographics can be charted on a 5 × 8 card, notebook insert, or similar format. Some instructional planners use a computerized data storage and retrieval scheme for their software. The areas that should be included are:

1. Objective(s)
2. Subject/topic
3. Grade/age level
4. Level of difficulty
5. Prerequisites
   a. Skills
   b. Other software
6. Hardware requirements
   a. Brand name
   b. Memory requirements
   c. Operating system
   d. Peripherals
7. Support materials required

Once the demographics have been written down, cross-referenced across main categories, and placed into a data retrieval or card catalog system, teachers will be able to find the programs they need to assist with the objectives their students are working on.

The performance criteria are the true evaluation for the software. Each is presented here as a category or a question. Some teachers will want to translate them into rating scales; others into brief comments. In either case, the user of these criteria will be holding the software up to close scrutiny.

Criteria 1: Directions. Good software programs are self-directing. The directions should be optional at the user's request and should be available on request for the user. Directions should include worked examples and should take the user through a sample activity.

Criteria 2: Instructional Organization. The way to look at instructional organization is to look at the software the same way we look at good teaching. In the classroom, we look at how materials are introduced, how appropriate the examples are, use of exercises and formative evaluation, sequencing, correctness of examples and facts, length of a lesson, and flexibility. Good educational software "acts like" good teaching. As teachers we try to be sensitive to our students' needs with regard to alternate examples, reteaching, and review. In computerized courseware, we call that "branching."

Branching should be evaluated. If a bright student is proceeding rapidly through the material, the program should skip ahead to a new section or another objective. If a student is struggling and missing all of the formative evaluation items, then that student's instruction should be switched and some sort of diagnosis performed. As we look at software, we need to evaluate the branching capabilities.

Criteria 3: Consistency. Good instructional software, like good teaching, is consistent. The screen layouts should be consistent throughout. The screens should also be uncluttered and self-explanatory. Question format and requests for input should be displayed in a consistent manner. If they are not, we may be putting a student through a screen deciphering exercise instead of a math or science lesson. Keystroke requests should be consistent. If some questions require the student to hit 'return' or 'enter' while other questions require only a single keystroke, students may become confused. Some software will accidentally generate wrong responses if an 'extra' return is encountered while others will stop altogether. Teachers should be sensitive to keyboard inconsistencies and include them in their evaluation.

Criteria 4: Help Functions. Who has ever heard of a class where the students can't ask for an explanation or a book where the pages can't be flipped in reverse order? All good software has a built-in help library available for the student when needed. Tutorials should be built in so that the help is not merely a glossary of terms or directions.

Criteria 5: Error Handling. Users of programs will make accidental errors. Some, such as an unneeded return, have potentially disastrous results. Others, such as, type "yes" instead of "y" or visa versa, should be handled by the software. Kids like to put in extra spaces either before or after the words. Good educational software always accommodates extra spaces. When upper and lower case can be treated equally, they should.

Accidental breaks or resets should be trapped and ignored. Unreasonable responses such as "1000" in response to how many spelling words should be tried ought to be trapped and disallowed. Many younger students like to hold keys down for an inordinately long time. This error should be accounted for and the results ignored. Superior courseware protects a program's data during an accidental crash thereby allowing a restart for the students.

Criteria 6: Reactions to wrong student response. When students misunderstand or when they are not following directions, good teachers sense this and alter their teaching strategy. Good computer programs do the same.

These six performance criteria are intended to help teachers and others to critically evaluate educational software. In all cases, the overriding criteria should be: *Does this courseware behave according to the behavior of good teaching?*

Finally, I urge educators to copy and use the Software Evaluation Form on pages 60–62, which should help in systematically appraising any software being considered.

SOFTWARE EVALUATION FORM

Part I. Program Descriptors

1. Title: _____

2. Brief Description: _____

_____

_____

3. Length (in minutes): _____

4. Computer: _____

5. Memory/O-S: _____

6. Format (tape or disk): _____

7. Support Material: _____

_____

_____

8. Subject: _____

9. Topic: _____

10. Grade level: _____

11. Level of Difficulty (high, medium, or low): _____

12. Objectives: _____

_____

_____

13. Prerequisites: _____

Comments:

Part II. Instructional Applications

(5 = always appropriate, 1 = never appropriate)

		Circle one			
1. Drill and practice	1	2	3	4	5	NA
2. Skill maintenance	1	2	3	4	5	NA
3. Review of facts	1	2	3	4	5	NA
4. Tutorial	1	2	3	4	5	NA
5. Concept introduction	1	2	3	4	5	NA
6. Concept reinforcement	1	2	3	4	5	NA
7. Small–group activity	1	2	3	4	5	NA
8. Large–group/class activity	1	2	3	4	5	NA
9. Simulation	1	2	3	4	5	NA
10. Experimentation/demonstration	1	2	3	4	5	NA
11. Data manager	1	2	3	4	5	NA

Comments:

Part III. Presentation Quality

(5 = outstanding, 1 = poor)

		Circle one			
1. Screen layouts	1	2	3	4	5	
2. Consistency of formats	1	2	3	4	5	
3. Content accuracy	1	2	3	4	5	
4. Directions	1	2	3	4	5	
5. Clarity of format/question	1	2	3	4	5	
6. Length	1	2	3	4	5	
7. Use of graphics	1	2	3	4	5	NA
8. Use of sound	1	2	3	4	5	NA
9. Error trapping	1	2	3	4	5	

Comments:

Part IV. Instructional Quality

(5 = outstanding, 1 = poor, 0 = does not exist)

Circle one

1. Appropriateness of content		1	2	3	4	5
2. Appropriateness of examples		1	2	3	4	5
3. Appropriate level of difficulty		1	2	3	4	5
4. Sequencing of examples/questions		1	2	3	4	5
5. Help functions	0	1	2	3	4	5
6. Use of formative evaluation	0	1	2	3	4	5
7. Branching	0	1	2	3	4	5
8. Quality of test items	0	1	2	3	4	5
9. Number of items/questions		1	2	3	4	5
10. Use of review	0	1	2	3	4	5
11. Introduction	0	1	2	3	4	5

Comments:

III. Implementing Computers

8. MECC: A Statewide Model for Educational Computing

Kenneth E. Brumbaugh

THE MINNESOTA EDUCATIONAL COMPUTING CONSORTIUM (MECC)[1] was created by the four public educational systems in Minnesota to coordinate and provide computer services to over a million students, teachers, and educational administrators throughout the state. It transcends the various organizational levels of education by serving elementary, secondary, vocational-technical, and higher educational institutions.

In MECC's coordination role, it has maintained a long-range master plan and a biennial plan for educational computing in the state, and reviewed and assisted institutions in developing annual computer plans. In its service role, MECC operates a statewide timesharing network, develops and implements computer-based management information systems, acts as a broker for similar services from member institutions, supports the acquisition and operation of microcomputers, and contracts for computer equipment that can be used by its members.

The Consortium's advisory structure consists of a Planning and Budgeting Committee and a Facilities and Services Review Committee, which is responsible for reviewing all proposals for computer services. Additionally, there have been a number of standing user advisory committees and periodic ad hoc task forces. MECC contracts annually

---

[1]The Consortium includes the Minnesota State University System (seven campuses), the Minnesota Community College System (18 campuses), the University of Minnesota (five campuses), the State Department of Education (433 school districts), and the State Department of Administration.

with its educational systems to provide specific services. The level of services and amount of contracts are fixed prior to the system's funding request to the state legislature. These agreements provide around 80 percent of MECC's total annual budget of approximately $7 million.

Instructional timesharing service fees are billed to the school districts at a fixed annual user charge per terminal access. Funding for special projects comes from federal and private sources.

MECC is divided into three operating divisions. The Instructional Services Division, the largest, manages and operates the MECC Timeshare System (MTS), a Control Data CYBER 170/720 with 375 user ports. At present, approximately 2,000 MTS computer terminals are located across the state in most public schools, all community colleges and public universities, and many of Minnesota's private schools. MECC personnel serve the users at all educational levels by conducting workshops, producing curriculum materials, training teachers, and teaching courses on instructional computing. They also provide written materials ranging from newsletters to curriculum guides for using computers in the classroom. A large multiplexing communications network provides the means by which users access the MTS computer. MECC has a program library of over 1,000 timeshare and microcomputer programs that supplement curricula at the elementary, secondary, and college levels. These programs have been developed by MECC staff and the MECC user community.

The Management Information Services Division performs tasks related to the development and implementation of management information or administrative data processing services for elementary, secondary, and vocational school districts. The services are provided through several regionally-based service centers located throughout the state. Comprehensive and flexible software has been developed and is being supported and maintained to support the school district management, data processing, and reporting needs in the areas of personnel, finance, student and instructional management. This software operates on the Burroughs B6800 series of computers.

The Special Projects Division initiates, implements, facilitates, and manages unique activities related to the use of computers in education. In carrying out its responsibility for project development, Special Projects staff participate in activities ranging from the initial exploration of a potential computer use to the implementation of major outside funded projects. Research projects designed to explore a wide range of hypotheses related to computer use in education are conducted by this division. Primary support for recent research has come from the National Science Foundation and the National Institute of Education.

Microcomputer Evolution

Through the MTS network, MECC has provided instructional timesharing services on a statewide basis since it was established. In 1977, MECC staff and users became aware of the potential of the microcomputer to provide many of the applications available on the MTS computer. They also became aware of the decreased costs of microcomputers coupled with their increasing capabilities; the rapid growth of microcomputer use in a variety of fields; and the potential elimination of dependence on the MTS network.

In order to meet the needs of instructional computing uses and to initiate an orderly, cost-effective process for delivering microcomputer services, a seven-member Instructional Task Force was established in January 1978. This group, which represented a variety of educational MECC users, was charged with the following objectives.

1. To conduct a survey for assessing the current and future microcomputer uses and needs of MECC users.

2. To determine the strengths and weaknesses of microcomputer use in various instructional computing modes and environments.

3. To provide demonstrations of microcomputer use for instructional purposes.

4. To coordinate and disseminate information regarding pilot programs using microcomputers.

5. To prepare recommendations regarding the potential for large-scale acquisition and utilization of microcomputers and the appropriate roles and responsibilities for MECC.

On the basis of a needs definition, the data collection, and a survey of current microcomputer users, the task force made the following recommendations:

• One specific microcomputer system should be available to all Minnesota education agencies and institutions through a state contract.

• Instructional service support for selected microcomputers should be defined and increased to the same level as was then available for large time-share systems.

• MECC should continue to analyze and evaluate microcomputer hardware and software technology, and disseminate information to the Minnesota educational community.

The MECC Board of Directors adopted the recommendations. In October 1978 MECC and Apple Computer, Inc. signed a contract for Apple's 32K, disk-based Applesoft microcomputer system.

Since 1978, approximately 100 microcomputers have been purchased each month by schools, colleges, and universities in Minnesota.

As of October 1981, more than 2,800 Apple II™ microcomputers had been ordered through MECC and installed in Minnesota's educational institutions. The amount of instructional timeshare system usage and the number of microcomputers within the MECC member system is shown by year in Figure 1.

Figure 1. Instructional Computing Growth in Minnesota

Year	Total # of Timeshare Terminals (est.)	# of Timeshare Ports Available	# of Microcomputers Obtained Through MECC	Total # of Microcomputers (Estimated)
1966–67	6	3	—	—
1967–68	15	5	—	—
1968–69	30	10	—	—
1969–70	65	25	—	—
1970–71	150	65	—	—
1971–72	245	108	—	—
1972–73	400	150	—	—
1973–74	500	210	—	—
1974–75	950	404	—	—
1975–76	1200	582	—	—
1976–77	1500	678	—	—
1977–78	1800	703	—	50
1978–79	2000	693	442[1]	517
1979–80	2100	714	914[1]	1556
1980–81	2200	781	944[1]	2925
1981–82	2150	724	800[2]	3875

[1]Apple II Microcomputers
[2]Apple II and ATARI Microcomputers (Partial Year)

Courseware Development

MECC User Services has been responsible for the initial development of courseware, computer software, and related materials developed for the Apple II microcomputer. The 11 professional staff members in this group spent approximately 40 percent of their time over two years developing, coordinating, or providing technical assistance to users related to the development of courseware. They also converted

Apple II as used in this chapter is a trademark of Apple Computer, Inc. ATARI is a trademark of ATARI, Inc.

many of the MTS programs to the Apple II microcomputer. In the process of conversion, the programs have been enhanced to take advantage of Apple II's color, graphics, and sound features.

In early 1980, a new group in the Instructional Services Division was created, the Instructional Systems Development (ISD) group. The ISD staff have two major tasks: (1) to obtain, classify, and refine Minnesota instructional computing courseware materials, both computer programs and related user documents; and (2) to distribute MECC instructional computing courseware within and outside Minnesota. The refinement of courseware products is absolutely necessary because many authors of computer programs neither have the skills necessary to make their programs transportable, or time to prepare the necessary support documentation, nor desire to complete these laborious tasks. MECC experience shows that often as much time and as many people are required to standardize programming routines and to clean up software as was used to create the programs, and again as much time and resources are necessary to prepare the user support documentation. In preparing written documentation for ensuring effective instructional computing, MECC depends on the use of a modern word processing system.

The number of programs that have been developed, documented, and are being distributed through MECC by subject area are shown in Figure 2. A wide variety of programs in a number of subject areas has been developed. A complete list and brief descriptions of the programs are available from MECC.

These programs are stored in the MTS computer and are available to all Apple II microcomputer users who use the microcomputer as a terminal to the host. Programs are also disseminated through software exchanges where individuals copy sets of programs distributed by MECC staff. Through both of these means, a high percent of Minnesota Apple II microcomputer users have the most current version of MECC supported programs. In addition to the 334 supported Apple II microcomputer programs, several hundred other programs are now being developed and will be shared by the user community. These programs represent instructional modes similar to those available in the commercial marketplace. A recent survey by Jostad and Kosel (1980) showed that "drill and practice" and "tutorial" applications are the most common program types available today.

In order to expand the distribution channels for microcomputer courseware, MECC adopted policies that allow the following methods for distribution:

1. Unit (single diskette or user document) sales by MECC to Minnesota customers at cost of production.

2. Unit sales by MECC to non-Minnesota customers at cost of production plus a development and administrative surcharge.

3. Institutional distribution agreements whereby nonprofit educational agencies outside of Minnesota can obtain an annual license to distribute MECC courseware to their own clientele.

4. Unit sales by commercial vendors of MECC courseware.

Figure 2. MECC Apple II Diskettes

Area	Diskettes	Programs
Agriculture	1	2
Art	1	5
Business	3	25
Elementary	14	80
English	1	7
Guidance	1	1
Instructional Management	1	1
Mathematics	5	41
Miscellaneous	1	5
Music Theory	1	18
Programming Aids	3	22
Programming	2	56
Science	4	26
School Utilities	2	6
Social Studies	2	13
Special Needs	1	1
Spelling	1	1
Teacher Utilities	4	19
	48	334
Plus diskettes for training materials	7	
Total:	55	

Comparison of Timeshare Computing and Microcomputing

As MECC prepared to blend MTS and microcomputing support for instructional computing users in Minnesota, it was necessary to review the actual user requirements regarding computer characteristics desired by users and instructional modes. Figure 3, which shows appropriate matches between these two variables, also serves as a guide for identifying which computer delivery system is optimum for various characteristics and modes of instructional computing.

Figure 3. Instructional Computing Requirements

IMPORTANCE	CHARACTERISTIC	CMI	Data Analysis	Drill	Information Retrieval	Materials Generation	Problem Solving	Programming	Simulation	Testing	Tutorial
HIGH	Ease of Use	X		X	X		X		X	X	X
	Reliability			X			X	X		X	X
	Responsiveness			X			X	X	X	X	
	High Student Terminal Time			X							X
	Accessibility	X		X			X	X	X		X
	Feedback	X		X	X		X	X	X	X	X
	Printed Output		X		X	X	X	X			X
	Graphics	X	X	X	X		X		X	X	X
	Large Data Source	X	X		X	X			X	X	
	Student Record Keeping	X		X							
	Multiple Languages			X				X			
	Large Amount of Text		X		X	X					X
LOW	Sound			X							X

X indicates which characteristics generally are requirements for the modes of use.

The computer characteristics listed in the left column of Figure 3 were rated for their importance from a user perspective and are listed from most important (top) to least important (bottom). 'Ease of Use' and 'Reliability' were judged to be the most critical user characteristics. Although not judged to be very important by itself, "Printed Output" was considered to be necessary for the most modes of instructional computing.

Using the data from Figure 3, MECC was able to forecast whether general purpose timesharing or microcomputing best served either the user characteristics as shown in Figure 4, or the mode of instructional computing as shown in Figure 5 on page 72.

Figure 4. Instructional Computing: Optimum Delivery System (Characteristic)

CHARACTERISTIC SYSTEM	General Purpose Timesharing	Microcomputing
Ease of Use		X
Reliability	X	
Responsiveness		X
High Student Terminal Time		X
Accessibility		X
Feedback		X
Printed Output	X	
Graphics		X
Large Data Source	X	
Student Record Keeping	X	
Multiple Languages	X	
Large Amount of Text	X	
Sound		X

X indicates which computer generally best fulfills requirement.

In order to complete the analyses shown in Figures 4 and 5, it was necessary to make different assumptions for each figure. To prepare Figure 4, the data in Figure 3 were summarized with the assumption that various modes of computer usage are best handled by either timesharing or microcomputing.

To prepare Figure 5, the data in Figure 3 were summarized with the assumption that certain computer characteristics are provided best by either timesharing or microcomputing.

By 1981 MECC had become solely a service organization devoted to responding to the needs of individuals, institutions, and agencies who sought instructional computing assistance. A long-range planning project completed in the spring of 1981 pointed to the need for new services. The changes were classified in two ways, those that had occurred prior to the beginning of the 1981 school year, and those that would occur during that school year. The two basic changes were:

1. The Minnesota State Legislature decided to appropriate significantly less revenue during 1981–83 for the support for the instructional telecommunications network; and

2. MECC decided to support a third computing alternative, a low-cost microcomputer.

Figure 5. Instructional Computing: Optimum Delivery System (Mode)

SYSTEM / MODE	General Purpose Timesharing	Microcomputing
CMI	X	
Data Analysis	X	
Drill		X
Information Retrieval	X	
Materials Generation	X	
Problem Solving		X
Programming		X
Simulation		X
Testing	X	
Tutorial		X

X indicates which computer generally best serves that type of usage.

During the 1981–82 school year, MECC would have to make two important decisions: (1) whether and how to extend the Apple II microcomputer purchasing arrangement; and (2) how much timeshare service was needed for MECC users and how to provide such service during the 1982–85 period.

The result of these changes would have significant implications for all Minnesota instructional computing users. The cost for the various instructional computing alternatives would change; in some cases upward and in some cases downward. Minnesota users would have to make a careful study of not only how much computing they need, but what types of computing service would be required to meet their needs.

Summary

The state of Minnesota recognized the need to cooperatively plan and coordinate the use of computers in education. To this end, it established a statewide consortium governed by representatives of the public education systems. Since it was established in 1973, MECC has provided statewide timesharing services, operated regionally-based educational management information centers, and conducted a number of research studies related to educational uses of the computer.

With the advent of the microcomputer, MECC recognized its potential and facilitated its use by schools, colleges, and universities throughout the state. Specifically, MECC established a statewide contract for acquisition of Apple II and ATARI microcomputers, provided training on their use, and developed and distributed courseware for classroom applications. This level of support has resulted in the use of approximately 4,000 microcomputers by over 350 educational institutions in the state.

MECC recognizes that although its approach has been successful, it may not be transportable to other regional, state, or national groups. Economic, philosophical, and technical considerations may determine the optimal approach to be used by others.

Bibliography

1979–80 Microcomputer Report of the Minnesota Educational Computing Consortium, May 1980, St. Paul, Minnesota (no longer in print).

Instructional Microcomputing and Timesharing: A Minnesota Perspective—The Report of the MECC Instructional Services Long-Range Planning Project, June 1981, St. Paul, Minnesota.

Jostad and Kosel, "Survey of Commercial Software," *AEDS Monitor* (Winter 1980).

9. TCEA: A Statewide Computer Education Association

Lyndal R. Hutcherson

BEGINNING AS AN IDEA FOR BRINGING TOGETHER PEOPLE WITH INTERESTS IN computers in the schools, the Texas Computer Education Association (TCEA) was started in 1980. James Poirot of North Texas State University organized the first meeting and hosted the first general conference where a steering committee was formed to write a constitution and bylaws. Formal adoption of the constitution and bylaws and election of officers was completed at the first annual meeting in the summer of 1980.

Administrative Organization

Since grass roots support of an organization is essential, TCEA formed five regional divisions within the state from which two representatives of each area were elected to serve on the board of directors. The positions of president, vice president, secretary-treasurer, and past president were also filled. The board of directors simply drew straws to determine if the first term of office would be for one or two years.

Membership and Dues

Regular and associate membership categories were created and annual dues set at $10.00 for each group. As an optional part of membership, the organization offered a subscription to The Computing Teacher as an added attraction. Also at their first meeting, the board of directors elected to join the International Council for Computers in Education (ICCE).

74

Purpose

The bylaws outline the purposes of TCEA, which are:

1. To encourage an active interest in computer education on levels K–12 throughout the state of Texas.

2. To provide an opportunity to study and keep abreast of new trends in computer education.

3. To improve teacher training programs in Texas in computer education.

4. To promote professional cooperation and communication between teachers and administrators toward the realization of sound educational achievements.

5. To provide a liaison with other organizations involved in the use of computers as an educational tool.

Area directors were encouraged to organize workshops and meetings in their own regions. Through such meetings, the directors could disseminate information from the state organization and communicate with area educators on computer needs. These meetings have been very well attended.

Membership in TCEA grew from approximately 100 at the close of the first annual meeting to nearly 1,000 by September 1982. TCEA newsletters had gained in popularity, evidencing the hunger of educators around the state for up-to-date information about computers and the use in the classroom.

The Second Annual Meeting

Austin, which is centrally located in Texas, was selected as the site for the second annual meeting, held in February 1982, 17 months after the first meeting. Twenty-seven speakers participated in the program. As a result of the enthusiasm of those who met in Austin, the board of directors decided that the third meeting would be advertised to the entire professional population in Texas. Not only would TCEA gain in strength, it would gain the support necessary for meeting the expanding needs of Texas schools.

Plans for the Future

In 1982, TCEA voted to create a joint committee with the Texas Association for Educational Data Systems to promote computer literacy in the state. TAEDS had issued a position paper on computer literacy and sought the support of TCEA in promoting computer literacy in the schools and, in particular, to the state board of education.

Association members have repeatedly cited a need for additional software for use in classrooms; the availability of good educational software is lagging behind the development of hardware. Although the Association has not yet adopted a formal plan of action, it has gathered approximately 300 programs for possible dissemination to TCEA members.

The present leadership of TCEA believes the Association will have a significant impact on many aspects of computer related instruction in Texas classrooms in the future. TCEA's newsletter,* regional workshops, and annual statewide meetings have already helped advance computer literacy in the state. The Association will continue to play an important role in the professional lives of its members—teachers, curriculum workers, and university professors throughout the state.

---

*To obtain copies of the TCEA newsletter and constitution, write to Dr. Lyndal R. Hutcherson, President, Texas Computer Education Association, 2800 Arcadia, Carrollton, Texas 75007.

IV. Computer Literacy
for Teachers

10. Teacher Competence: What is Needed

M. Tim Grady and James L. Poirot

As WE MOVE TOWARD EXTENSIVE USE OF COMPUTERS IN SCHOOLS, we see a major problem: teacher computer literacy. The definition of "computer literacy" varies among educators. In a practical sense, we can expect most educators to want to define computer literacy in terms of the competencies to be acquired. A lot of school administrators, university professors, and other professionals (including a subcommittee of ACM, the Association of Computing Machinery) have begun to list competencies and suggestions about training and curricula. As those of us who are close to the question of how and what to teach teachers try to organize and implement staff development plans for teachers, we must know what these competencies are.

Required Competencies

The following lists include the competencies that a major portion of the education community should possess.

Administrators

School administrators—assistant superintendents, supervisors, consultants, principals, and others—should be "literate" in the areas of their responsibilities. Most of these areas involve the selection and purchase of hardware, software, and staff development materials. Seldom do they need to be programmers.
1. Computer terms and definitions
2. Computer systems
3. Word processing uses and limitations
4. Data-based management systems

5. Budget analyses via electronic spread sheets
6. CAI and CMI applications, examples, and limitations
7. Software evaluation procedures
8. Hardware evaluation and selection procedures
9. Research efforts and results for computer uses in schools

All teachers

All teachers should attain a certain level of computer literacy. We frequently hear the argument that all students should be computer literate. A logical extension of that thought is that teachers should be on equal footing with the kids. Teachers in general should have an understanding of the capabilities, uses, and limitations of computers. The following competencies should be included in any citation of computer literacy for all teachers.

1. Computer systems
2. Computer terms, jargon, and colloquialisms
3. Educational, albeit instructional, uses of computers
4. History of computers and calculating
5. Problem-solving techniques; computers and problem solving
6. Nonschool uses of computers
7. Relationships between society and computers

Computer teachers

We must expect those who teach about computers to attain the same level of competence as all teachers in general, and to possess special competencies of their own. Those competencies should be more than just programming skills; the computer teacher must have current knowledge of computer applications and the state of the art of technology. Computer teachers will be resources for other teachers, parents, and students from a variety of disciplines. They may also be resources for the principal who seeks to use computers for administrative purposes. Thus, computer teachers must attain the following competencies.

1. Competencies cited for administrators and for all other teachers
2. Programming skill in more than one computer language
3. Knowledge of the capabilities of the operating system for the hardware in the school
4. Knowledge of and ability to teach problem solving
5. Knowledge of computer system architecture (a) in general, and (b) in the specific sense of the hardware in use

6. Knowledge of communication and networking hardware and software architecture

7. Knowledge of a wide range of standard algorithms commonly employed on computer systems

8. Software evaluation skills

Definitions of Competencies

Computer systems. Knowledge of the major components of a computer system. Ability to explain the function of the different components in a system and their relationship to each other. An understanding and ability to explain how a "job" is processed by the components of a system. Knowledge of the different types (alternatives) of any one of the major components of a system, such as printers, disk drives, and processors.

Computer terms and definitions. Ability to explain the meaning of the common terms and names used in computer science.

Word processing. Knowledge of what word processing is. Familiarity with most common packages, their advantages and limitations, and applications in school settings. Familiarity with comparison criteria for evaluating new word processing software.

Educational uses of computers. Knowledge of the uses and limitations of computer-assisted instruction, computer-managed instruction, tutorials, simulations, and teacher management tools.

Data-based management systems. Ability to define the term data-based management systems (DBMS). Familiarity with main products available for one's own hardware. Ability to establish criteria for selecting a DBMS, and knowledge of possible applications of a DBMS—attendance, inventories, student records, and so on.

Software evaluation skills. Ability to assist in evaluating, selecting, and developing appropriate instructional materials that use microcomputers.

Hardware evaluation and selection procedures. Ability to evaluate hardware systems on the basis of (1) software compatibility, (2) memory requirements, (3) external storage needs, (4) printer needs, (5) anticipated expansions, and (6) purchase and maintenance costs. Ability to write bid specifications and to evaluate the written bids of hardware vendors.

Knowledge of system architecture, communication, and networking. Ability to explain, discuss, and analyze a hardware configuration that employs (1) a networking scheme, or (2) communication software and hardware including modems and protocols, or (3) a variety of peripheral devices.

Problem-solving techniques; computer problem solving. Knowledge of and ability to teach classical five-step problem solving, and to apply problem-solving techniques to software problems.

Research results in the use of computers in schools. Knowledge of results of studies on the effects of computer use in schools and ability to interpret results in light of local needs and educational objectives.

Nonschool uses of computers. Familiarity with and understanding of the most common uses and applications of computers outside the school environment—including research, arts, weather, government, defense, medicine, libraries, law enforcement, and others.

Relationships between society and computers. Knowledge of the impact of computers and technology on our society, including the dangers of misuse of databases, and privileged information. Ability to increase students' awareness of these relationships.

Programming and algorithm skills. Ability to write computer programs that are correct and well-documented within a reasonable length of time. Knowledge of a range of standard algorithms, including I/O routines, sorting procedures and applications, debugging procedures, file structures, use of compilers, and use of operating systems and system libraries.

By themselves, the above competencies are insufficient. We need comprehensive programs at both the preservice and inservice levels. Preservice programs must exist within the traditional teacher education programs and address certification requirements as well as degree requirements. Competencies should be translated into teacher training for the regular classroom teacher and the computer teacher.

Inservice education is presently required of just about all teachers. The need for well-defined programs in this area is urgent, since many teachers are being pressed into teaching computer science without the benefit of formal training in the discipline. The competencies set forth in this chapter must be translated into staff development programs for our present teaching and administrative staffs. Much work remains to be done.

Bibliography

An Agenda for Action. Reston, Va.: National Council of Teachers of Mathematics, 1980.

Atchinson, William F. "Computer Science Preparation for Secondary School Teachers." *SIGCSE Bulletin* 5 (1973): 45–47.

Conference on Basic Mathematical Skills and Learning. U.S. Department of Health, Education and Welfare, Euclid, Ohio, 1975.

"Curriculum '78: Recommendations for the Undergraduate Program in Computer Science." Report of the ACM Curriculum Committee on Computer Science, December 1978.

Danver, Jean H. "Suggestions for Programs." Hanover, N.H.: Keiwit Computational Center, Dartmouth College, 1970.

Dennis, J. Richard; Dillhung, C.; and Muiznieks, J. "Computer Activities in Secondary Schools in Illinois." *Illinois Series on Educational Applications of Computers, No. 24.* University of Illinois, 1977.

Esterson, D. M. "Problems of Implementation: Courses of Pre- and In-Service Education." *Information and Mathematics in Secondary Schools.* North-Hollard Publishing Company, 1978.

Fetcher, L. "What is an Appropriate Way to Teach Educators About the Uses of Computers?" Paper presented at the National Educational Computing Conference, Kansas City, 1982.

Horn, C., and Poirot, J. L. *Computer Literacy.* Swift Publishing, 1981.

Moulton, Peter, and Moursund, Davis. "A Summer Master's Degree Program in Computer Science." *Topics in Instructional Computing SIGCSE* 1 (January 1975): 31–36.

Poirot, James L. *Computers and Education.* Swift Publishing, 1980.

Poirot, James L. "A Course Description for Teacher Education in Computer Science." *SIGCSE Bulletin* 8 (February 1976): 39–48.

Poirot, James L., and Groves, D. N. *Beginning Computer Science.* Manchaca, Texas: Sterling Swift Publishing, 1978.

Poirot, James L., and Early, G. G. "Teacher Certification—A Computer Science Necessity." *Topics in Instructional Computing SIGCSE* 1 (January 1975): 15–18.

Poirot, J. L.; Powell, J.; and Taylor, Robert. "Teacher Education." *Topics: Computer Education for Elementary and Secondary Schools SIGCSE-SIGCUE Joint Issue* (January 1981).

Recommendations Regarding Computers in High School Education. Washington, D.C.: Conference Board of the Mathematical Sciences, April 1972.

Science and Engineering Education for the 1980's and Beyond. Washington, D.C.: National Science Foundation and Department of Education, 1980.

Shotwell, S. "Quality Inservice Training." Paper presented at the National Educational Computing Conference, Kansas City, 1982.

Spencer, Donald. "Curriculum and Teacher Training for Secondary Schools." *Interface* 5 (April 1972).

Statz, Joyce. "Training Secondary School Computer Science Educators." *Topics in Instructional Computing SIGCSE* 1 (January 1975): 4–9.

Taylor, Robert P. "Graduate Remedial Training in Computing for Educators." *SIGCSE Technical Symposium Proceedings,* Dayton, Ohio, February 1979.

Vockell, E.; Rivers, R.; and Kozubal, D. "Computer Literacy for Teachers: An Intensive Program." Paper presented at the National Educational Computing Conference, Kansas City, 1982.

11. Training Teachers to Use the Powerful Tool

Sandra K. Pratscher

PICTURE THIS SCENARIO. The PTA of a small-town elementary school has decided to donate a microcomputer system to the second-grade class. The parents, convinced that the school needs a computer, raise funds for purchasing the system. The computer arrives. The children are delighted and anxious to learn. The teacher is nervous and just plain anxious.

This scene is familiar to educators working in schools today. Inservice instructors are facing a great challenge. They are being asked to deal with a technology that simply did not exist when they were learning to teach. And they're being asked to use a tool whose potential and promise only a few among us have begun to imagine.

Teachers, as a group, are very much aware of the need for computer-related training. In a survey conducted by the Minnesota Educational Computing Consortium, 85 percent of 1,300 teachers agreed that secondary school students should have minimal understanding of computers. However, only 39 percent agreed that their own training was adequate for using computers in instruction. And in central Texas, requests for computer-related training are so great that more teachers are turned away than can be served.

How are we to bridge this teacher-training gap? How can careful planning precede the use of computers so that teachers are given the information and support they need? What is the role of the school's instructional leader in providing that training? To answer these questions, it is crucial that planners of computer-related inservice sessions for teachers first consider how this training differs from other types of inservice training.

We must recognize that for the first time educators have access to an instructional tool that has more than a single purpose. In the past, instructional tools were designed essentially for single, specific tasks—film projectors for running movies, overhead projectors for showing images on a wall, and so on. We now have a tool for instruction that is not only something we can teach with and use for many purposes, but also something we need to teach about. Computers in school are bound to affect the way we teach almost every conceivable subject.

Deliverers of inservice training must be careful about the language they use. Most teachers do not yet speak "computerese," and a highly technical vocabulary intimidates them. By the same token, talking down to teachers is insulting. Trainers must also realize that many teachers are machine-anxious, an attitude perpetrated by machine-anxious administrators, especially those whose PTAs have donated systems. In any case, some teachers may actually need to be desensitized while others may only need encouragement. This anxiety about hardware, by the way, is not peculiar to teachers; it appears that anxiety level may be more a result of one's age than one's profession. As one computer instructor noted recently, "When you give adults an unfamiliar gadget, they'll look at it and think, 'My God! I'll break it!' But a kid will look for the on/off switch."

While trainers need to be sensitive to teachers' emotional reactions to the computer and structure the training in a nonthreatening atmosphere, it is possible to give teachers false impressions. Consider, for example, the trainer who begins by telling teachers that a computer system is no more difficult to operate than an overhead projector. Ms. Jones, trusting the trainer, believes what she hears. Her first encounter with the machine yields, "Syntax error in line 150." As a result, Ms. Jones is convinced she's a hopeless computer illiterate since she can't operate a tool as simple as an overhead projector. Thus, the trainer must be supportive yet honest about the fact that the computer is a very sophisticated problem-solving tool, and to use it effectively requires time and effort.

In "hands-on" training (a requirement of all but awareness sessions), educators must experience some degree of success in at most 30 minutes. If not, learners will become frustrated and have difficulty progressing. Trainers should begin with short, simple exercises and move to more complex examples only after initial success has been achieved. All adults must have a way of saving face, and it is helpful to use programming assignments, for instance, that have sample solutions on the back.

Individualized work in a session should be preceded by some group instruction. Most adults feel comfortable with lecture-oriented instruction since most of their school learning began that way. When participants do begin to work independently, the trainer should remain close at hand (at least initially) to help with questions.

Teachers must be shown that the computer can help them—that it can be used to generate printed material, including worksheets and tests, and to assist in the multitude of paperwork teachers are required to do.

Training should also be directly tied to the level of teachers' use. Teaching computer mathematics in high school requires a very different set of skills from those required to run a science simulation with 5th graders. This, of course, means the trainer must have a defined set of competencies around which to plan each session.

Those of us who have "gotten religion" about instructional computing tend to be rather evangelical about the technology and its implications for teaching. Still, we must keep in mind that it is a mistake to pack too much information into too short a time frame. People can assimilate only so much in a given time period; they need more time to practice new ideas and adapt them to their personal needs.

Finally, teachers must be given honest information about the computer's promise for the future. They should not be led to believe the computer is a panacea for curing all the ills of education.

Suggested Training Sessions

I. BASIC Programming (2 to 3 days)

Description. This is a workshop designed for the novice adult. Each morning is spent in group instruction, with each new concept demonstrated on a computer system. We use either a large screen for output or a network of several systems. Beginning commands and statements are introduced and participants given time to work on practice assignments (both pencil-and-paper and on-line). At the end of each day, they work on simple problems to practice using BASIC as a problem-solving tool (for instance, compute the value of the change you have in your purse or pocket.)

Rationale. I have a "gut" feeling that all educators who are new users of computing systems have at least some notion of how to communicate with the system and how to use the language of the system in problem-solving applications. When their initial experience is with "canned" software, they may not have the pleasure of communicating with the system in a way that allows them to be in charge and solve problems they want to solve. We run a grave risk if we only show teachers (and students, for that matter) how to use software, and never have them use a high-level language in a problem-solving context.

Suggested materials:

(a) *Hands-On Microcomputer Workbook and Courseware* by J. Poirot and D. Retzlaff. The courseware is a set of programs that are loaded into the computer and used to teach the BASIC programming language. Courseware and workbook are intended to be used together. No prior programming experience is necessary. Initial programs show how the keyboard is operated; final programs illustrate advanced programming applications.

Published by Sterling Swift Publishing Company, P.O. Box 188, Manchaca, Texas 78652. Cost: $69 for courseware (diskettes or tapes for Apple, TRS 80, PRT, or TI 99/4). $5.95 for workbook.

(b) *Teaching BASIC Bit by Bit* by B. Friedmann and T. Slesnick. Set of lesson plans for an 8-day, 12-hour course in BASIC, using Apple computer systems. Appropriate for ages 10 to adult and contains activities for Apple and PET. Published by Math and Co. Puter Education Project, Lawrence Hall of Science, University of California, Berkeley, California 94720. Cost: $9.00

(c) *BASIC Discoveries* by L. Malone and J. Johnson. Book presents BASIC programming through an exploratory and problem-solving approach. Activities may be reproduced for participant (or student) use. Published by Creative Publications, P.O. Box 10328, Palo Alto, California 94303. Cost: $7.50

(d) *Overhead Masters for Teaching BASIC* by D. Spencer. Book provides masters for introducing BASIC statements and commands, as well as excellent sample programs for each new idea. Useful for group instruction segment of the workshop. Published by Camelot Press, P.O. Box 1357, Ormord Beach, Florida 32414. Cost: $4.50.

II. Computer-Assisted Instruction: Definition and Use (1 to 2 days)

Description. In this session, we discuss and demonstrate each of the standard kinds of computer-assisted instruction, including drill and practice, tutorial, simulation, problem solving, games, testing and evaluation, diagnosis, and prescription. As each prototype is discussed, instructional setting considerations are addressed. Participants receive assistance in planning both pre- and post-interaction activities for students.

Rationale. This workshop addresses the use of computers as instructional media to support traditional content. We find that many schools (especially elementary) first become involved in instructional computing using this application. The problems, of course, are lack of quality software support and lack of sufficient hardware. Consequently, we emphasize two points in this session: (1) how school personnel can locate good quality instructional software and integrate it into traditional instruction, and (2) how a system can be used to serve a maximum number of students.

The Minnesota Educational Computing Consortium is the best single source of good quality instructional software. However, we find that teachers need a good deal of assistance in planning for integrated use of that software. They need to consider appropriate pre- and post-interaction activities; whether an interaction should involve individual students or group instruction; which students are likely to benefit from which kinds of interactions; how to manage students on and off the systems (mainly how to get their darling hands away so that another may have a turn); how to integrate computer-assisted instruction with other instructional activities—and the list goes on and on. In other words, we encourage teachers to view CAI as an important adjunct to instruction, rather than as a filler that students use at the back of the classroom when they've finished their other work. Our concern is that educators may miss a significant opportunity if students see CAI as something not tied to a particular learning objective.

Suggested materials: Minnesota Educational Computing Consortium software.

III. Computer Assisted Design (1 to 2 days)

Description. Group I—Design in BASIC: For participants who are comfortable with BASIC programming, we discuss good design considerations (short text with frequent interactions) and share with them subroutines that are useful with CAI programming (checking routines, routines for providing positive feedback, and so on). Group II—Design in an authoring language: Some teachers are interested in designing programs for students, but don't feel comfortable enough with BASIC to develop an instructional package. We cover the same design considerations as in the BASIC Design Workshop, but use popular authoring systems instead of a traditional high-level language.

Suggested materials:

(a) *Design and Development of Computer Based Instruction* by G. Culp. This book will be published soon as *An Apple for the Teacher.*
(b) Apple Pilot
(c) TRS 80 Pilot

(d) Genis

(e) Aristotle's Apple

IV. Planning for the Use of Computers in School (½ day)

Description. This workshop is generally addressed to administrators to help them plan carefully before purchasing hardware. We follow a system-analysis approach in which we identify needs and match them with computer resources.

Rationale. Many school leaders who purchase hardware without looking at needed applications end up disappointed in what they buy and disenchanted with educational computing. Schools can avoid such problems by having a written plan of action before implementing an instructional computing system.

Suggested materials:

(a) *School Administrator's Guide to Instructional Use of Computers* by D. Moursund. Published by ICCE, c/o Computing Center, Eastern Oregon State College, LaGrande, Oregon 97850. Cost: $2.50.

(b) *Guide for Selecting a Computer-Based Instructional System* by the Texas Education Agency Computer Task Force. Published by Texas Education Agency, 201 East 11th Street, Austin, Texas 78701. Cost: Free.

V. Computer Literacy (1 to 2 days)

Description: This workshop includes both an elementary and a secondary session and covers the history of computers; computer terminology; hardware components; the impact of technology on society, career, awareness; computer systems and structure; computer architecture; algorithm development and flowcharting; computer logic (some Boolian algebra); and computer-related numeration systems. The presentation of each concept includes both content and suggestions for delivering content to students. Good classroom activities must be a part of the activities of this session.

Rationale. More and more teachers need help in teaching young people about computing, and students need more than just BASIC programming skills. Unfortunately, many teachers are expected to incorporate computer literacy into the curriculum for students when they themselves have had little or no exposure to that content. Thus the trainer in a computer literacy workshop must not only deliver content, but also provide ideas for student activities dealing with content. Learning about computing is more than learning the syntax of a programming language. It involves learning a whole range of new ideas, new problem-solving techniques, new communication methods, and new ways of thinking about the world.

Suggested materials:

(a) *Flowcharting* by J. D. McQuigg and A. M. Harness. Published by Houghton Mifflin, 12400 Midway Road, Dallas, Texas 75234. Cost: $4.50.

(b) *What Do You Do After You Hit Return?* by People's Computer Company. Published by Hayden Book Company, Rochelle Park, New Jersey. Cost $14.95.

(c) *Computer Literacy Show and Tell Kit* by J. Poirot. Published by Sterling Swift, P.O. Box 188, Manchaca, Texas 78652. Cost: $59.95.

(d) *Be A Computer Literate* by M. J. Ball and S. Charp. Published by Creative Computing Press, P.O. Box 789-M, Morristown, New Jersey 07960. Cost: $3.95.

(e) *My Friend the Computer* by Jean Rice. Published by Math-Master, P.O. Box 310 M, Big Springs, Texas 79720. Cost: $3.95.

(f) *Are You Computer Literate?* by K. Billings and D. Moursund. Published by Dilithium Press, P.O. Box 92, Forest Grove, Oregon 97116. Cost: $5.95.

(g) *IPC Paper Computer Simulator* by F. C. Matt. Published by Instructo/McGraw Hill, Paoli, Pennsylvania. Cost: about $10.00.

VI. Software Selection and Evaluation (1 day)

Description. We present participants with evaluation forms or assist them in developing their own. Most of the day is spent helping participants evaluate software and locate specific software packages for desired uses.

Rationale. For awhile instructional computing consultants blamed lack of software support for problems in implementing computers in schools. Now, however, it often seems that far too much software is available. Few school people have the time or expertise to wade through the incredible bulk of products on the market and determine which package is most appropriate for specific instructional uses. We try to assist school personnel in making software decisions by showing them how software can be evaluated. We rely on EPIE and MicroSIFT for assistance and use their instruments for the majority of the evaluations we conduct.

Suggested materials:

(a) *NCTM Guidelines for Evaluating Computerized Instructional*

Materials by W. P. Heck, J. Johnson, and R. J. Hansky. Published by the National Council of Teachers of Mathematics, 1906 Association Drive, Reston, Virginia 22091. Cost: $3.75.

(b) *Scholastic Microcomputer Instructional Materials.* Published by Scholastic Software, 904 Sylvan Avenue, Englewood Cliffs, New Jersey 07632. Cost: Free.

(c) *Educational Software Directory.* Published by Sterling Swift, P.O. Box 188, Manchaca, Texas 78652 D. Cost: $14.95.

V. Computer Literacy for Students

12. Comprehensive Planning for Teaching About Computers

Ronald E. Anderson

VERY LITTLE SYSTEMATIC TESTING HAS BEEN DONE ON WHAT STUDENTS KNOW and feel about computers. The two noteworthy exceptions are the 1978 National Assessment of Educational Progress and the 1979 state assessment in Minnesota. From the national assessment in 1978, we can make the following relevant conclusions:

● Access to computer facilities is rather low. Only 12 percent of junior high (13-year-old) and 25 percent of senior high (17-year-old) students indicated they had "access to a computer terminal to learn mathematics."

● Very few claim to be able to program a computer. Only 8 percent of the 13-year-olds and 13 percent of the 17-year-olds said they could write a program.

● Only 11 percent of the 17-year-olds reported having had some coursework in computer programming.

The test results from both the National Assessment and the Minnesota assessment warrant the following additional conclusions:

● Performance on flowchart reading exercises and simple BASIC programs reveals very poor understanding of algorithmic processes involving conditional branching.

● About half of the students who have taken computer programming classes are still unable to read a simple flowchart.

● A few of the students who have taken computer programming classes seem to have little or no understanding of general computer capabilities, even though students in general, even those lacking computer experience, seem to have such an understanding.

● Many students, both with and without computer programming coursework, do not seem to have a sense of the value of computers for themselves personally or for society.

• Major disparities in opportunities for becoming computer literate exist in our society. These inequities are greatest for racial and religious minorities; however, in some instances, students who are female or who live in small communities are also disadvantaged.

These conclusions pose a serious challenge to the educational system. Correcting inequities and deficiencies will require a major commitment to an extensive, comprehensive program of computer literacy in elementary and secondary schools. Before discussing the ingredients of a curriculum that would solve these problems, it would be well to first review what computer literacy is all about.

Computer Literacy

An argument for the comprehensive perspective on computer literacy has been set forth by Anderson, Klassen, and Johnson (1981), who contend that computer literacy is an understanding of computers that enables one to evaluate computer applications as well as to do things (such as program) with them. The opposing view is that computer literacy is simply a matter of doing things on a computer.

The comprehensive view of computer literacy is consistent with the current recommendations of the National Council of Teachers of Mathematics (1980). In "An Agenda for Action," NCTM recommends that "A computer literacy course, familiarizing the student with the role and impact of the computer, should be a part of the general education of every student." Moursund (1976), Rawitsch (1978), and Watt (1980) all define computer literacy in a broad, comprehensive fashion. There are very good reasons for people to be able both to communicate with computers and to be knowledgeable about them.

In defining computer literacy it is useful to distinguish it from computer science. The most succinct distinction is that computer literacy is the part of computer science that everyone should know or be able to do. Both language literacy and scientific literacy are commonly defined in terms of the layperson and his or her needs. Computer literacy should be thought of as the knowledge and skills the average citizen needs to know (or do) about computers. This obviously implies that students should be taught more than simply how to operate or program a machine. They also need to know how computers can be productively used and what the consequences of computerization are. Thus matters of computer literacy should be taught not only in the mathematics department but in science and social studies courses as well.

Ordinary people, old and young alike, have very real, practical needs for computer understanding. For example, all of us need to know enough about computer systems so as not to be intimidated by a computerized billing error; we need to know whether or not to acquire computer equipment for home or work; we need to know how to judge whether computer applications are helpful or harmful; and so forth. Some of these things can be learned as a byproduct of learning to write simple BASIC programs; but most of this useful knowledge cannot be learned that way. Most of what every ordinary citizen needs to know about computers will not be learned from learning how to program. Other types of instruction must be provided as well.

A K–12 computer literacy curriculum must encompass (1) programming and algorithms, (2) skills in computer usage, (3) hardware and software principles, (4) major uses and appropriate applications, (5) limitations of computers, (6) personal and social uses, and (7) relevant values and attitudes.

One serious problem is that in the brief time of a typical course, the student can learn very little about problem solving and algorithms, to say nothing of the other topics and domains listed above. To accomplish reasonable goals for a comprehensive computer literacy curriculum, it is imperative that computer information be infused into the traditional content of many different courses. In addition, a one- or two-term computer literacy course should be introduced into the curriculum of the junior high school. Finally, computer literacy courses should be required for all students, not just the gifted ones.

One component of this comprehensive computer literacy course should be computer programming. To avoid the problems that have been associated with typical BASIC programming courses, a more complete approach to programming is needed. An elementary introduction to an algebraic language, such as BASIC, PASCAL, or FORTRAN, is useful for teaching the concepts of replacement, iteration, selection, and input/output. This work can be supplemented with a procedure-oriented language such as LOGO, with special emphasis on the structure of algorithms.

Whatever programming languages are taught, the emphasis must be on designing modular solutions to practical problems. One such approach would be to build the course around a table calculating language such as VISICALC.[1] Not only will students learn some important programming concepts, but they will develop skills in organizing information and personal planning and problem solving.

---

[1]VISICALC is a trademark of Visicorp.

If students do not learn word processing or text editing in other classes, the computer literacy course should introduce them to some text editing tasks so that they can learn some skills for enhanced writing and gain an improved appreciation for the application of computers in word processing.

Another problem in teaching comprehensive computer studies courses is that computer programming activities tend to engulf the attention of both students and teachers. Social issues are likely to be scheduled for the end of the term when little or no time is left for them. Computers and social issues, sometimes called "awareness" issues, should be introduced on a regular basis throughout the course, and wherever possible integrated with hands-on computer activities. For instance, a text editing exercise can be followed by a unit on the impact of word processing on society.

Unfortunately, the approach suggested here is not yet fully embodied in any published course materials. The Minnesota Educational Computing Consortium is currently in the process of developing a series called Computer Literacy Instructional modules (CLIMS).[2] Numerous other course materials are anticipated during the next few years.

Whatever is developed and adopted will have to be periodically revised because new computer equipment and software tools will become available. The educational system has an obligation to teach students those techniques that are current and useful to them in their roles as students and citizens. For example, keypunching does not need to be taught anymore, but data entry skills, including typing, should be taught to every student. Only a few students will become data entry clerks, but every student will need to be able to use a keyboard in order to keep up with the computerized society of the next two decades. Many recently published courses in keyboarding attest to this emergent curricular need.

Many educators do not yet realize that recent microcomputer software has transformed the computer into an indispensible personal tool for the average citizen. Word processing packages and table calculating languages (such as VISICALC and SUPERCALC), to say nothing of entertaining games and educational coursework, make microcomputer systems compelling for every home and classroom. A computer system with such an array of software, including a printer,

---

[2]For information on CLIMS, contact Ronald E. Anderson, Minnesota Center for Social Research, University of Minnesota, 2122 Riverside Avenue, Minneapolis, Minnesota 55454.

can be purchased for considerably less than $2,000. An ideal classroom/laboratory for a computer literacy course would have about ten such systems so that every two or three students would have access to a machine.

Why should every student be given learning opportunities on computers? Because they embody the current major personal (including educational) applications of the microcomputer. Students who are being trained to become effective citizens must be taught more than how to write their own simple BASIC programs. They must know what such systems have to offer and how to evaluate their usefulness to their individual needs.

At the present time, while not all households can afford these systems, household members are nonetheless in need of computer learning because they are likely to encounter computer activities at work. Workers are increasingly being placed in a computer "work station" environment where they have computing machines on their desks to use in writing, organizing, and planning, which have access to large, remote data files. Students need the skills and confidence necessary to deal with computerized work environments as well as their own personal, computer-related decisions.

Obviously the approach proposed here cannot be successfully implemented without a strategy for training teachers. Teachers cannot be effective unless they are abreast of the current developments in personal and instructional computing. Allowing teachers to take microcomputer systems home and encouraging home computer activities such as word processing and home budgeting will foster informal learning. Other approaches, such as formal coursework, inservice workshops, and computer delivered refresher courses, should be planned as well. But the key to a worthwhile teacher training program is an adequate, well-conceived incentive system.

References

Anderson, Ronald E. "National Computer Literacy, 1980." Paper presented at the National Computer Literacy Goals for 1985 Conference, Washington, D.C., December 1980.

Anderson, Ronald E., and Klassen, Daniel L. "A Conceptual Framework for Developing Computer Literacy Instruction." *AEDS Journal* (Spring 1981).

Anderson, Ronald E.; Krohn, Karl; and Sandman, Richard. "User Guide for the Minnesota Computer Literacy and Awareness Assessment." St. Paul: Minnesota Educational Computer Consortium, 1980.

Carpenter, Thomas P., and others. "The Current Status of Computer Literacy: NAEP Results for Secondary Students." *Mathematics Teacher* (December 1980): 669–673.

Johnson, D. C.; Anderson, R. E.; Hansen, T. P.; and Klassen, D. L. "Computer Literacy—What Is It?" *Mathematics Teacher* (February 1980): 91–96.

Klassen, D. L.; Anderson, R. E.; Hansen, T. P.; and Johnson, D. C. "A Study of Computer Use and Literacy in Science Education, Final Report." St. Paul: Minnesota Educational Computing Consortium, 1980.

Moursund, D. "What is Computer Literacy?" *Creative Computing* 2 (1976): 55.

Papert, Seymour. *Mindstorms—Children, Computers, and Powerful Ideas.* New York: Basic Books, 1980.

National Council of Teachers of Mathematics. *An Agenda for Action: Recommendations for School Mathematics of the 1980s.* Reston, Va.: NCTM, 1980.

Rawitsch, D. G. "The Concept of Computer Literacy." *MAEDS Journal of Educational Computing* 2 (1978): 1–19.

Watt, D. H. "Computer Literacy: What Schools Should Be Doing About It." *Classroom Computing News* (December 1980).

13. Learning About Computers in Grades K-8

Beverly Hunter

COMPUTERS ARE TOOLS. AS INDIVIDUALS AND AS GROUPS, WE USE THESE TOOLS to handle information, communicate with others, and solve problems. Thus, computers are of value to students in their handling of information, communicating, and problem solving.

There is now a wide variety of computer-based tools available for student use. These include word processors, math-logic tools, simulations, and information retrieval programs. In this chapter we will look at some of the specific, practical uses of computer-based tools for K–8 students.

General Goals

While the comprehensive scope and sequence of computer literacy objectives[1] for grades K–8 is not the subject of this chapter, a general goal for *all* students is development of the ability (1) to use suitably programmed computers in appropriate ways to assist in learning and solving problems, and (2) to make informed judgments about social and ethical issues involving computers and communications systems. The key phrases here are:

- "ability to use" as opposed to, for example, "knowing about."
- "suitably programmed computers" as opposed to "computers."

This work was supported by the National Science Foundation, Grant No. SED79-23684.

[1]See Beverly Hunter, "Computer Literacy in Grades K–8." *Journal of Educational Technology Systems* 10 (1981–82): 59–65.

- "in appropriate ways," which implies the need to think critically about what is and is not appropriate.
- "to assist in learning and solving problems," which implies support for the purposes of schooling.

Word Processing Tools for Language Arts

The most widely used electronic tool to aid in writing communications is the word processor. A common misconception about word processors is that they serve only to make typing more efficient, which is not normally a goal of elementary school education. In actuality, word processors designed for school children can help them to learn and apply:

- the mechanics of writing (that is, typing),
- spelling,
- grammar and punctuation,
- the organization of ideas and information,
- the creative process of writing, and
- the editing and revision of compositions.

The word processor tool itself assists in teaching students that writing is an iterative process—that drafts contain errors in spelling, punctuation, grammar, and sentence construction, and that the organization of ideas requires improving. The tool, once mastered by the user, alleviates the mechanical drudgery of revising and rewriting. Thus the user is encouraged to continually revise and improve.

Word processing or language arts systems for children have such built-in features as:

- a typing tutor that gives timed exercises to build speed and accuracy on the keyboard;
- a spelling checker that warns when a word the child has written is not on the list of approved spellings;
- features for handling files, editing, and formatting that are easy to learn and do not require double and triple keystrokes;
- other aids, including stored formats for conventional forms such as letters and short stories, automated dictionaries, and sentence word-counts.[2]

---

[2]For a discussion of first-graders' use of stored formats, see Robert W. Lawler, "One Child's Learning: Introducing Writing With a Computer." *Siggue Bulletin* 14 (July 1980): 18–28.

Problem-Solving Tools for Mathematics

The highest priority recommendation of the National Council of Teachers of Mathematics is that problem solving be the focus of school mathematics in the 1980s.[3] Computer literate students will use the computer as a tool to execute problem-solving procedures. The student analyzes a problem, develops a sequence of steps for solving it, and tells the computer to carry out the problem-solving steps. The student then studies the results and determines whether the outcome or solution is the intended outcome. If it isn't, the student must re-examine the procedures and revise them.

In order to use the computer in this way, the student must learn to use the appropriate software or "math-logic tools," although that phrase isn't exactly descriptive. A good example of an appropriate tool is LOGO;[4] another is PILOT; but many other tools are being developed. Using Univers' "mapper" system, for instance, students can see mathematics represented in visual graphic form. Thus they can apply mathematical representations to sets of objects, dimensions of objects, and lines, distances, speeds, locations, time, direction, sounds, and so forth. The visual or sound representation provides a more intuitive and concrete experience for the child than does a purely mathematical or verbal representation.

Curriculum designers and teachers need to find or devise collections of problems that will help students discover and apply the particular mathematical skills and concepts that the curriculum calls for. Because of the power of the tools, students can solve more complex problems than are practical with only pencil and paper. As a result, some math objectives will need to be covered earlier in the curriculum. For example, a student who is writing procedures to generate geometric forms may first need to learn formulas for computing areas and perimeters. Ideas about variables, how to use and name them, are also needed earlier. The new math of the 1960s includes variables as boxes and triangles with relatively little difficulty.

Simulations for Science and Social Studies

Eventually, children's versions of computer-based tools now used by professionals and scientists will be integrated into the science

---

[3]National Council of Teachers of Mathematics, *An Agenda for Action: Recommendations for School Mathematics of the 1980s* (Reston, Va.: NCTM, 1980).

[4]Seymour Papert, *Mindstorms* (New York: Basic Books, 1980).

classroom. These include instruments and programs for capturing data in the laboratory or natural world, programs for analyzing and storing data, systems for retrieving data and scientific literature, programs for playing "what if," and simulations.

Although simulations are among the most important kinds of computer-based tools used in natural and social sciences, their application in the elementary classroom is as yet primitive and poorly understood. There are two interrelated reasons for using simulations in elementary science. One is to aid in understanding natural phenomena. The other is to learn about simulation and problem solving—how to use, criticize, modify, and improve a simulation for a particular purpose. To use a simulation effectively, the student must learn systematic strategies for exercising the simulation. For example, students begin to explore relationships among variables by varying only one parameter at a time and holding all others constant. Students also need to criticize simulations—for example, identifying real world variables that are not taken into account in a particular simulation.

A danger in overuse or misuse of computer simulation is the introduction of too abstract a model before the student has acquired prerequisite experience with physical, concrete phenomena. Effective use of simulations need to be combined with hands-on laboratory and field activities. For example, the lesson plans for using the simulation "Compete"[5] combine laboratory exercises in growing real plants with use of a simulation of plant competition.

One way to avoid the danger of students using computer models they don't understand is to have the students themselves develop the models. Abelson and Goldberg of MIT have developed a LOGO-based curriculum unit that shows students how to create LOGO turtle simulations of the behavior of mealworms. "What is important is that the students *themselves* design the experimental models, and not merely supply parameters to a preprogrammed simulation."[6] Students move back and forth between activities with live mealworms and their own simulations of the mealworms.

Social Studies

Computers are not just personal tools. Computer systems are as interwoven into the fabric of our society as automobiles, books, and

---

[5]"Compete" (Iowa City: Conduit, 1981).

[6]H. Abelson and P. Goldenberg, "Teachers' Guide for Computational Models and Animal Behavior" (Massachusetts Institute of Technology Artificial Intelligence Memo No. 432, April 1977).

laws. "Computers shouldn't be studied in isolation, but should be integral parts of larger social systems."[7] Social studies should provide computer literacy with regard to:

- social responsibility and values
- decision-making skills
- use of information in a democratic society
- impact of technology historically and in the future[8]

Issues of social responsibility, ethics, and values with regard to information and systems are of greatest concern. Many issues of rights and responsibilities in data access need to be understood. Values such as privacy may conflict with other values such as lower crime rates. What about ownership of data, trade secrets, patents, and copyrights? What about the professional obligations of computer scientists? How do professional groups decide what is ethical? Some computer software could be so bad that its release and sale is unethical. What if a software bug—a kink in the program—causes the death of a hospital patient or a plane to crash? Whose responsibilities are these? How does the use of large computer-based systems affect accountability of people for their work? Is it accurate to say the computer caused a problem? Or did the programmer cause it? Or did the person who directed the programmer cause it?

Such issues, considered on a national or international scale, may seem too abstract for elementary and junior high students. But student use of computer-based tools in school will generate many concrete case studies in ethics and values. The classroom and the school will become a microcosm of the larger society; many social issues can be addressed at this more concrete level. If I copy someone else's program and then modify it for my own use, am I "cheating"? Or are we "collaborating"? If our class is creating a data base of geography information, how do we make sure erroneous information doesn't get into it? Is someone responsible for the accuracy of the data base? If I write a report that depends on information I got from your data base, how can I be sure your information is correct?

Learning materials, lesson plans, and text materials on such topics are nonexistent at the K–8 level, although many excellent texts exist at

---

[7]Report of Working Group IX, "Computer Literacy in the Social Studies Curricula" in *Computer Literacy: Issues and Directions for 1985*, eds. R. E. Anderson and B. Hunter (New York: Academic Press, 1982).

[8]Richard A. Diem, "Computer Literacy in the Social Studies Classroom," in *Computer Literacy: Issues and Directions for 1985*, eds. R. E. Anderson and B. Hunter (New York: Academic Press, 1982).

the college level.[9] A challenge for the curriculum designer or teacher will be to translate adult and college-level materials into a relevant context and concept level for junior high students.

Procedural Thinking

Students must be able to develop, test, debug, and use problem-solving procedures in order to use computer-based tools. A procedure is a description of how to do something. It is a specific set of instructions that must be carried out in a specified sequence. A procedure might be spoken, written, acted out, or depicted with pictures or flowcharts. The way in which a procedure is designed and written depends on who is going to carry out the procedure. Often when we tell a person how to do something, we can be a little sloppy in our description because we can depend on the person to figure out what we mean. When we tell a machine how to do something, however, we must be far more careful and precise because the machine is far more limited in its intelligence and vocabulary. This general principle applies whether we are making entries in a computerized cash register, using a word processor, playing electronic "Star Wars," writing programs in BASIC, or doing multiplication on a calculator.

Students learn and apply the concepts and skills involved in procedural thinking in at least three ways:[10]

1. By describing a familiar activity in terms of procedures. Students learn to make descriptions at the appropriate level of detail, making sure the activity is completely described in the correct sequence of steps since the procedure must be carried out literally. Students test and debug their procedures by having a partner carry out the procedure and watching the results.

2. By using or modifying a procedure for solving a problem in math, social studies, science, or language arts. This differs from the common classroom practice of following directions—"Now do this; now do that." Instead, they are provided with a complete procedure that has a name, a beginning, and an end. Their attention is directed to

---

[9]"Computers and Privacy" study unit (Boulder, Colo.: Biological Sciences Curriculum Study, 1980); J. Weizenbaum, *Computer Power and Human Reason* (San Francisco: W. H. Freeman Co., 1976); and Donald Sanders, *Computers in Society* (New York: McGraw Hill, Inc., 1981).

[10]I wish to acknowledge the contributions of Dan Watt, formerly of the MIT LOGO Laboratory; David Moursund of the University of Oregon; and Kay Morgan, formerly of the Montgomery County, Maryland, Public Schools, in the formulation of these ideas on procedural thinking.

the usefulness of the procedure for accomplishing a particular task, rather than focusing solely on getting the correct answer.

3. By developing procedures to solve new kinds of problems and deciding what tools are most appropriate to use. Would it be best to use a paper-and-pencil procedure? A procedure that uses a calculator? A procedure that uses a computer program? The student may break up the problem into subproblems and develop a procedure for each subproblem.

The abilities both to use and to develop procedures are the most fundamental and important prerequisites to becoming "computer literate." Procedural thinking will become more and more a formalized component of the curriculum and classroom methods in all basic subject areas.

Library Media Skills

Just as students need to be able to find and use appropriate books in the library, they need to be able to locate and use appropriate programs and documentation. This means, for example, that the student must be able to use documentation to decide whether a given program is suitable for the purpose at hand, and how to load and operate the program.

Ability to locate and retrieve information from computer data bases will be as basic as the ability to use an index or table of contents in a book. Though few elementary school students now have access to data bases appropriate to their studies, there are some data bases available. For example, Tell Star[11] is used to selectively retrieve information about stars, planets, and constellations; and Supermap[12] for retrieving facts about states and cities. Provided with appropriate software tools, students can build their own data bases and use them in class projects.

State of Our Knowledge

Almost no formal research or evaluation has been conducted or reported on:

● the kinds of cognitive skills students develop when they use the kinds of tools discussed here;

11"Tell Star" (Berkeley, Calif.: Information Unlimited Software, Inc., undated).
12"Supermap" is a product of Apple Software.

- how to teach children to use such tools;
- affective and social implications;
- benefits, limitations, and risks associated with the uses of these tools;
- implications for curriculum goals and objectives;
- costs to society of providing these tools for children; costs of not providing them.

Implementation

The software, lesson plans, and teacher training needed to implement the curricular innovations discussed here have not been fully developed. How then might a school or school district go about the process of implementation? I suggest the following five steps.

1. Place initial emphasis on getting procedural skills integrated into all subject areas and grade levels. This does not require equipment.

2. Have a microcomputer available in the school library media center, with as wide a variety of software as possible. Select the micro on the basis of the software tools available. Spend as much money and research effort on software as on hardware.

3. Continue a focused, directed search for software tools that can be used by students and teachers. These might include authoring systems such as PILOT; math-logic systems such as LOGO; data management programs; simulations; text editors and word processors; information retrieval systems.

4. Encourage and support the innovating, self-motivated teacher to try out the use of these tools in the classroom. Conduct carefully monitored, small-scale experiments with such classroom use. Don't try to involve all teachers at this stage.

5. Select an application that has been assessed, on the basis of classroom experience, as being clearly beneficial to students. Then plan how this application can be integrated into the curriculum for all students and teachers for whom it is relevant. Lesson plans, teacher training, software, equipment, administrative support, and assessment methods should all be included in this plan.

As more and more students begin using computer-based tools, we will need to re-examine goals, objectives, and sequencing of curricula in basic subjects. Handwriting, spelling, arithmetic computation, memorization of facts, are all areas that may be de-emphasized in favor of problem solving, information handling, experimentation, and greater social interaction.

14. The High School Computer Science Curriculum

M. Tim Grady

THE NATURE OF A HIGH SCHOOL COMPUTER SCIENCE CURRICULUM is very different from traditional subjects because it lacks a history. Mathematics, physics, and English, for example, are school subjects tied to a discipline and to college entrance requirements. Computers are a relatively new kid on the block. Hence, we curriculum workers are left on our own to develop a meaningful course. The result has been that schools have developed computer science courses that differ on almost every criteria. This chapter sets forth two frameworks for high school computer science curriculum.

The modern electronic computer has its origins in the search for assistance in making large, fast calculations. Prominent scientists and mathematicians such as Von Neuman were among the pioneers in the field. Many of us still think of the computer as the tool of mathematicians. True, computers serve mathematicians and scientists well, but they have their widest applications in the areas of business data processing. Each and every one of us is affected by the large scale data processing in our routine daily operations. School curriculum workers need to face up to the fact that the most common uses of computers in our society exist in nonscientific environments. Hence, our curriculum for teaching about computers should reflect the reality of how computers are most frequently used.

Computers should be used to support instruction in a wide range of subjects, especially in mathematics and science. However, when teaching *about* computers, the course should stand on its own two feet and not be part of any traditional department. In cases where the school must place the course within a department, the most appropriate is the business education department.

Figure 1
Outline of High School Computer Science Course Content

I. Literacy
   A. Vocabulary
   B. Applications
   C. System Architecture
II. Using a Computer
   A. Data Base Management
      1. Inventories
      2. Mailing Lists
      3. Sort Routines
      4. File Maintenance
      5. File Transfer/Backup
      6. Report Generation
   B. System Operation
      1. O/S Protocols
      2. Passwords and Security
      3. Systems
      4. Batch Processing
      5. Priority Assignment
      6. System Utilities
   C. Elementary Programming
      1. Generalized Algorithms
         a. I/O
         b. String Manipulation
         c. Sorts
         d. Loops
         e. File Structures
      2. Use of Compilers
   D. Use of Standard Packages
      1. Business Operations
         a. Payroll
         b. General Ledger
      2. Accounting Spread Sheet
      3. Word Processing
   E. Communications
      1. Hardware
         a. Modems
         a. Multiplexers
      2. Protocols
      3. Public Data Bases
         a. BBS Services
         b. The Source
         c. Bison

A well-rounded computer science course must necessarily be much more than computer programming. Figure 1 outlines a typical computer science course. As in other subject areas, motivation to participate is a major problem for the teacher. Luckily, the computer teacher has an advantage over most other subject area teachers in that students can experience almost immediate success, the salient variable in the motivation equation. By using existing serious programs, such as an inventory package, students can create a list of their friends, catalog cars, or make a personal electronic phone book. All beginning computer courses should begin with the use of existing applications software. The motivation to learn "how that works" can be quite powerful.

The computer curriculum should reflect the fact that many of today's job applicants need to know how to use computers in an applications setting. Students who work through our curriculum should be competent in system operations and the use of sophisticated software such as data based management systems, electronic spread sheets, and word processing. The second and third sections outlined in Figure 1 detail the nature of this suggestion.

Programming skills are, of course, part of any good computer science curriculum. The emphasis should be on learning standard or commonly used algorithms. Wherever possible, programming should be language independent. Because this is not possible in most settings, teachers should make every effort to show students that some techniques are almost always used in the same way regardless of the programming languages that are available.

Our society is rapidly becoming engulfed by information. Ways of dealing with the information explosion are being examined and tried out—via cable TV, public data bases, computer networks, and a variety of telecommunications phenomena. A good high school computer science course should include a study of the communications hardware and software that students will likely encounter in the workaday world.

Computer Math/Programming Course

Many schools have computer math classes and do not teach computer science as discussed above. Figure 2 sets out an outline for a good computer programming course. Unlike the computer science course, the programming course emphasizes the technical and analytical skills necessary to be considered competent in computer programming.

The key ingredient in a programming course is that it revolves around algorithmic thought. Standard or common techniques should be mastered in at least two languages. Means of interfacing with system programs and system libraries must be learned. A final must is a good understanding of file structures and common file handling procedures.

Figure 2
Outline of High School Computer Programming Course Content

I. Terminology and Background
II. Algorithmic Thought
  A. Basic Concepts
  B. Task Analysis
  C. Flow Charting
III. Computer Languages
  A. Machine Code
  B. Assemblers
  C. Higher Level Languages
  D. Compilers and Interpreters
  E. System Languages
IV. Programming Principles
  A. Instruction Sets; Syntax
  B. Character Types
  C. Counters
  D. I/O Demands
  E. Branching
  F. Loop
  G. Sorts
  H. Subroutines
V. File Structures
  A. Sequential Files
  B. Relative Files
    1. Index Files
    2. Pointers
  C. Transaction Files
VI. Advanced Topics
  A. Subscripts
  B. Standard Techniques
    1. Bubble Sorts
    2. Shell-Metzner
    3. Tree Sorts
  C. Library Routines
  D. Graphics
    1. Memory Mapped Video
    2. Paper Graphs
    3. Plotters
    4. Sealing Techniques
VII. Interface Routines
  A. I/O Routines
    1. Handshaking
    2. Peripheral Drivers
VIII. On-Line Techniques
  A. Menus
  B. Program Modules
    1. Linking
    2. Branching

    C. System Calls
    D. Relocatable Subroutines
    E. Customization Techniques
IX. Gaming and Stimulation
    A. Learning Programs
    B. Artificial Intelligence
    C. Interactive Video Games
    D. Inferential/Prediction Simulation

Teachers of programming courses should choose their exercises very carefully. Examples should be used from a variety of disciplines. Science provides many good iterative problems while business provides good file manipulation studies. The use of alpha characters in sorting routines as well as report generation is essential to a programming curriculum. These examples can be taken from familiar school examples such as scheduling, attendance, book inventories, and sports statistics.

Teaching Programming to Gifted Students

The limited scope of most high school programming courses, together with limited amounts of equipment and teachers with a noncomputer background, pose a problem for the few truly gifted students. Most schools are unable to provide an adequate course for them. What schools should provide in these cases is "opportunity," not curriculum. Opportunity is defined as plenty of time on the computers during noncomputer class time, access to complete manuals, and lots of reference material. Grades should not be a consideration for the gifted computer student. Suggested projects might include a check-in/ check-out system for the school library, a student scheduling system, the invention of a word processor, modification to a computer operating system to make it more friendly, a textbook inventory program, a basketball or baseball statistics and recordkeeping program, an accounting package for the school newspaper and/or annual staff, a program for nonprogrammers that writes programs, or a program to score a yachting regatta.

High school curriculum workers should keep an eye toward the real world as they build a computer science curriculum. Programming is an important part of computer science, but is not equivalent to computer science. The suggestions made here are intended to help curriculum workers make reasonable plans as they work toward a computer curriculum.

VI. Computer Uses
by Subject Area

15. Computers in Library Media Centers

Gerald Lundeen

THERE ARE TWO PRINCIPAL WAYS IN WHICH COMPUTERS ARE USED IN LIBRARIES. The first, library automation, uses computers to perform many of the functional tasks involved in running a library. These kinds of applications have been made in many libraries over the past 20 years or more, though school libraries have not been as involved in computer use as have academic, special, and public libraries. The recent developments in computer technology have made it much more feasible for small libraries to consider automating many of their functions, and even to plan for a totally automated library.

The second application of computers in libraries serves a media function. This is a relatively recent phenomenon, largely associated with the introduction of low-cost microcomputer systems and courseware (software, workbooks, manuals, and so on).

Library Automation

The "housekeeping" functions in a library include circulation control, cataloging, acquisitions, serials control, film and other media booking, and the production of management information. These operations involve many repetitive clerical tasks that are especially amenable to automation. Justification for converting from manual processing to computer processing may be based on potential cost savings, improved service, new services, and combinations of these. Careful analysis and planning are required to assure that expected benefits are feasible and are in fact achieved.

There are three basic approaches to automating library processes: joining a network, buying a turnkey system (a hardware and software package), and developing a system locally.

112

In-House Development

The third option is very difficult to justify in any type of library and especially in the typical school library that does not have the staff and facilities for software development and hardware interfacing and maintenance.

There are times, however, when creating a system locally is the only choice—when no available system can meet your special needs and resources. This situation can generate a system that can later be marketed to other libraries with similar needs. For example, to replace its card catalog, the Mountain View Elementary School in Broomfield, Colorado, developed, with the help of a consultant, a microcomputer-based catalog that is now being marketed.[1]

Networks

Networking involves acquiring suitable equipment (typically a terminal and communications devices to connect to the telephone system) and arranging to participate in a library service located elsewhere and shared by other libraries. Networks may be local, perhaps connecting all schools in a district, or statewide, regional, national, or international.

Basically, networking for library functions involves sharing resources. Computer timesharing is one aspect of this. Many school districts operate a relatively large computer that is used in a timeshared mode by all of the schools in the district, not only for library applications but for administrative and instructional purposes as well. The Shawnee Mission (Kansas) Public Schools' library automation system is a notable example of the use of a large computer in timeshared mode to perform a variety of tasks—central library processing; data retrieval; automated acquisitions; production of catalog cards, microfiche union catalogs, bibliographies, and printed catalogs.[2]

A similar approach may involve groups of libraries using centralized processing facilities. Automated library systems may provide for sharing resources and effort among several types of libraries so that school, public, and academic libraries share common computing facilities. At the nationwide level, four major systems were originally organized for sharing cataloging data. These systems, generally referred

---

[1]Betty Costa, "Microcomputers in Colorado—It's Elementary!" *Wilson Library Bulletin* 55 (1981): 676–678, 717.

[2]Don D. Shirley, "Data Processing and School Media Centers," in *Today's Revolution: Computers in Education* (Washington, D.C.: Association for Educational Data Systems, 1976).

to as bibliographic utilities, are now evolving into total library services, providing acquisitions, circulation, interlibrary loan, and serials control. Of these, one is Canadian (UTLAS—the University of Toronto Library Automation System); one is regional, with the possibility of being duplicated in other areas (WLN—the Washington Library Network); one serves primarily the needs of academic and research libraries (RLIN—the Research Libraries Information Network); and one attempts to serve all types of libraries nationwide (OCLC, Inc.—the Online Computer Library Catalog, originally the Ohio Colleges Library Center). Both OCLC and WLN have been used by several school library media centers.[3]

The library media specialist should be aware of the computer-based acquisitions and cataloging services offered by some of the large book jobbers. These services allow on-line ordering and provide catalog card sets for purchased items.

Another type of network service is the provision of on-line access to bibliographic data bases. This service provides access via a computer terminal and telephone to a large number of databases containing citations to reports and published literature in almost all fields of knowledge. Of particular interest to educators is the ERIC database, which combines and cumulates the information published in *Resources in Education* and *Current Index to Journals in Education*. The three major vendors of this kind of service are Lockheed Information Systems' DIALOG system, System Development Corporation's ORBIT, and Bibliographic Retrieval Services (BRS). The librarian, using one or more of these services, can provide access to millions of citations to literature useful to students, teachers, and administrators. Articles or documents themselves can also be ordered through these systems if they are not available locally.

A new form of on-line computer service is represented by The Source and Compuserve. Many libraries are subscribing to one or both of these services, which offer a variety of information and assistance: movie reviews, electronic mail, airline schedules, games, wire service news stories, weather forecasts, and programming languages, to list a few.

[3]See, for example: Janet Alexander, "School Libraries and the InCoLSA Network," *Hoosier School Libraries* 16 (December 1976): 31–34; Paula N. Deal, "A Study of Centralized Processing for School Media Centers," *Drexel Library Quarterly* 13 (April 1977): 80–90; Audrey Kolb, "Development and Potential of a Multitype Library Network," *School Media Quarterly* 6 (Fall 1977): 21–27; and J. Steepleton and others, "An Introduction to OCLC and Its Application to School Media Centers," *Media Spectrum* 4 (1977): 23–24.

Turnkey Systems

Turnkey systems have in the past been designed to perform single isolated functions, such as circulation control. These are now evolving into multifunction, integrated library systems. Turnkey systems are, in general, based on minicomputers, or more recently on microcomputers, and are sold with the software to perform the initial functions. The availability of relatively low-cost microcomputer systems now makes it possible for libraries with small budgets to consider automation.

Circulation control is an application for which several turnkey systems have been available for several years. Many of these are evolving into on-line catalogs as well, and some are integrating other functions, such as acquisitions and serials control, resulting in total library systems.

It is possible to buy separate turnkey systems for several housekeeping functions. The library taking this piecemeal approach should pay particular attention to the compatibility of modules so that data generated in one function can be used in others. Likewise, the capability to link a turnkey system to a network should be considered when selecting a system.

Computers as Media

Computer-aided instruction has been practiced in many schools for several years, based on timeshared use of minicomputers or large mainframe computers, either locally owned or via a network.

The PLATO system, developed at the University of Illinois and marketed by Control Data Corporation, is an example of the shared use of large systems. The library/media center is a logical location for the terminals that are used to access timeshared systems.

The recent availability of low-cost microcomputer systems is attracting a great deal of attention from educators and librarians. These systems are being acquired by many schools and larger administrative units. Library media centers have traditionally been responsible for educational equipment, so it would seem reasonable for them to purchase, catalog, provide access to, and maintain microcomputers and their associated courseware. The location of microcomputers during use depends on their application; they may be portable and moved around as needed. Security must be considered due to the cost and portability of this equipment.

Microcomputers generally come with a limited amount of software—an operating system and one or more programming languages. This is sufficient for teaching programming, but for other applications additional software is needed. Educational software is available from a variety of commercial and noncommercial sources. Library media specialists, school teachers, and students may also develop their own. The area of microcomputer educational software is disorganized and largely centered around a cottage industry lacking standards, quality control, and direction. Programs vary widely in quality, and the accompanying documentation (instruction for use) is often inadequate. Costs vary from a few dollars to several hundred dollars for individual software packages, and may not be related to the quality of the program.

Evaluation of available software is not as well organized as the evaluation of books and other media. Occasionally, software packages are reviewed, but for the most part it is up to the library media specialist to evaluate the products.

The decreasing costs and increasing power of computers, together with an expanding choice of services, software packages, and turnkey systems, and the rapid evolution of microcomputers offer exciting possibilities for changing the way school library/media centers operate and how they serve their clientele.

Automation of the various housekeeping functions is now within the grasp of even small libraries through stand-alone microcomputer-based systems, vendor or cooperative network services, or regional cooperation with timesharing or centralized processing.

The availability of low-cost microcomputers offers exciting possibilities in computer-aided instruction and in increasing the level of computer literacy among students. Many good quality CAI courseware packages are available and more are being developed. Current efforts at identifying and evaluating this material should aid in the selection process.

The combination of microcomputers with videodisc and telecommunications technologies will certainly transform the school library/media center in many ways.

Sources of Further Information

Pierre Barrette, *The Microcomputer and the School Library Media Specialist* (Littleton, Colorado: Libraries Unlimited, 1981).

John Corbin, *Developing Computer Based Library Systems* (Phoenix, Arizona: Oryx Press, 1981).

Howard Fosdick, *Computer Basics for Librarians and Information Specialists* (Arlington, Virginia: Information Resources Press, 1981).

Franz J. Frederick, *Guide to Microcomputers* (Washington, D.C.: Association for Educational Communications and Technology, 1980).

Gerald Lundeen, "The Role of Microcomputers in Libraries," *Wilson Library Bulletin* 55 (November 1980): 178–185.

Joseph R. Mathews, *Choosing an Automated Library System: A Planning Guide* (Chicago: American Library Association, 1980).

Jennifer E. Rowley, *Computers for Libraries* (Sauer/Bingley, 1980).

Dan R. Twaddle, "School Media Services and Automation," *School Media Quarterly* 8 (Summer 1979): 257–268, 273–276.

16. Computer-Assisted Mathematics

Donald Piele

TO THE GENERAL PUBLIC, COMPUTERS ARE STRONGLY ASSOCIATED WITH mathematics and mathematicians. This connection stretches back to the very beginning of the concept of numbers and their representation by a physical thing—from a pebble to a bead on a wire, a mark on a piece of paper, the rotation of a mechanical wheel, to the state of an electrical relay, a vacuum tube, a transistor, and, now, of an integrated circuit on a single slice of silicon. The alliance between computing and mathematics is very real. Eminent mathematicians occupy critical positions on the list of men and women who have contributed to the advancement of automatic calculating machines.[1]

Ironically, the obvious computational power of the computer has led to some confusion about its use in the mathematics classroom. It is not uncommon to hear arguments that students will no longer need to develop computational skills if a computer "can do the work for them." At the other extreme, some teachers enthusiastically endorse the use of computers as a tool to individualize the teaching of computational skills. Both views place a heavy emphasis on the computational aspects of mathematics. But to mathematicians, the computational power of the

---

[1]Blaise Pascal invented the first machine capable of performing arithmetical functions; Gottfried Leibnitz created an ingenuous way to perform multiplication and division mechanically. Charles Babbage devised the analytical engine, generally recognized to be the first programmable computer. Ada, Countess of Lovelace, worked with Babbage, ultimately creating the complete specifications for his general purpose computer. Howard Aiken originated the idea of using magnetic relays to construct a general purpose computer. John von Neumann contributed the concept of a stored program, a major step in the development of computers. Stanislaw Ulam invented the Monte Carlo method for finding solutions to mathematical problems by random sampling with a computer. John Kemeny co-authored the BASIC computer language. Patrick Suppes pioneered the development of CAI. John McCarthy developed the LISP language. Seymour Papert directed the creation of the LOGO language.

computer has always been viewed as a service to the primary function of mathematics—problem solving. A common thread running throughout the work of the mathematicians who contributed to the development of computers is the desire to relegate to a machine the bookkeeping and computational chores that impede the creative work that humans do best, solving problems.

Problem Solving—Today

Teachers of mathematics recognize the importance of problem solving in their field. In its recent report, *An Agenda for Action*, the National Council of Teachers of Mathematics (NCTM) (1980) identified the improvement of problem-solving skills as its primary objective for the 1980s. In a separate PRISM study (Priorities in School Mathematics), problem solving—the development of methods of thinking and logical reasoning—was identified by 95 percent of the teachers responding as the most important objective in the teaching of mathematics (NCTM, 1981).

But in reality, students spend nearly all of their time today getting ready for problem solving. The first six years of mathematics in our schools are devoted to learning the four basic functions: addition, subtraction, multiplication, and division. So much time is spent mastering these computational skills that almost no time is left for actually solving problems.

Problem Solving—Tomorrow

The use of computers in the classroom will bring, in the next ten years, increasing pressure for change in the mathematics curriculum. Specifically:

1. Computational activities will be handled more and more by the computer.

2. Software packages that extend the user's ability to investigate nonroutine problem-solving situations will replace many purely computational exercises.

3. Programs that place students in problem-solving environments, in which they can set parameters and make decisions while a computer reveals the consequences of their actions, will become part of the curriculum.

4. Mathematical programming—constructing algorithms and running them on a computer—will become an accepted part of the mathematics curriculum.

In general, the availability of inexpensive microcomputers will make it possible for students to use a computer as a partner in the problem-solving process. In some areas of the U.S. this is already being done.

Beyond CAI

Computer-assisted instruction, as traditionally conceived, has been one of the fondest dreams of educators. The possibility that the computer will one day make truly individualized instruction a reality seems reasonable enough. Unfortunately, CAI has so far proven more difficult to do well than was ever dreamed possible. As a consequence, programs ready for use today on microcomputer systems merely hint at the potential of which educators have dreamed. So what are teachers doing with their microcomputers today?

In 1975, a survey of secondary level computer usage (Burkoski and Korotkin, 1976) revealed the following mix of instructional computer activities:

Problem solving	25%
Programming	25%
Simulation and games	15%
CAI	13%
Guidance and counseling	15%
Other	7%

A 1980 ACM report on CAI in U.S. public secondary/elementary schools showed that 90 percent of all school districts are now using the computer for instructional purposes; teaching computer languages is the number one use; and mathematics has the highest priority (Chambers and Bork, 1980).

To the computer user, CAI and programming stand at opposite ends of the computer applications spectrum. The first use requires absolutely no knowledge about computers, while the goal of the second is a complete understanding of how to control computers. Between using the computer as a teaching machine and using it to learn BASIC lies a sleeping giant—computer-assisted mathematics (CAM).

Computer-Assisted Mathematics

The idea of using the computer to provide students with an algorithmic approach to mathematics and a chance to experience the problem-solving process firsthand is not new. Fifteen years ago, it was the major emphasis of a precollege program at the University of Minnesota, the Computer Assisted Mathematics Program (CAMP). The program produced six books, one for each grade level, 7–12, designed around the BASIC language in a timesharing environment. The authors gave careful attention to identifying particular problem-solving situations in which students could develop algorithms. The algorithms chosen were compatible with the mathematics curriculum of the grade level.

The results of the experiment, as reported by the authors, indicated that the computer was an invaluable device for demonstrating mathematical concepts. Also, the computer activities proved to be an excellent device for involving the students in problem solving. There were many instances in CAMP in which students were given the opportunity to design an algorithm, program it, and then run it on the computer. If it didn't work, the student revised the program and tried again until it "worked." This type of "real world" problem solving, which is difficult to implement successfully in the traditional textbook setting, was found to be inherent in computer problem-solving activities.

In the early 1960s when CAMP materials were being developed, the computer was not an easy tool to use. Programs were stored on punched cards and submitted to the computer in a batch mode. Modifying a program was a very time-consuming process. The availability of computers for high school students was limited and for elementary students completely nonexistent. In addition to these hardware limitations, the CAMP materials did not venture beyond the traditional mathematical algorithms found in textbooks. They did not introduce, for example, such programming strategies as recursion, backtracking, merging, sorting, and branching that are commonly used today to solve problems with the computer. As a consequence, programs like CAMP did not have a lasting impact on the mathematics curriculum of the day. It was viewed primarily as an enrichment activity.

Computer-Assisted Mathematics—The Future

It seems inevitable that the widespread use of computers in the classroom will ultimately have a significant impact on the mathematics curriculum, although the resulting design is difficult to forecast. The best we can offer is an approximation. Below is a list of distinct programming categories that are closely related to mathematical concepts and skills. Specifically, they include the ability to program a computer to explore and/or solve problems in the following categories:

I. Numbers
   a. Displaying patterns
   b. Transforming between bases
   c. Counting
   d. Searching for those that satisfy certain conditions
   e. Searching for those that have mathematical properties
   f. Sorting
   g. Shuffling
   h. Generating at random
   i. Coding and decoding

II. Words
   a. Concatenation and decomposition
   b. Counting
   c. Sorting
   d. Shuffling
   e. Transposing
   f. Coding and decoding

III. Simulation
   a. Games of chance
     (1) Coin tossing
     (2) Random drawings or movements
   b. Games of skill
     (1) Board games
     (2) Strategy games

IV. Problem-Solving Skills
   a. Backtracking
   b. Bisection
   c. Recursion
   d. Subgoals
   e. Trial and error

V. Graphics
   a. Plotting
   b. Geometric designs

All of these activities depend on and reinforce portions of the traditional mathematics curriculum. Examples of the kinds of programming problems that fall into these categories are widely available.[2] None of these sources has, however, developed materials to a point at which they could be easily used in a computer-assisted mathematics classroom. At present these materials are primarily for enrichment activities.

The development of a well-defined and interesting computer-assisted mathematics curriculum is a long-term project and will not happen overnight. It will require the combined efforts of teachers, students, and curriculum developers working together to make it happen. No matter how long it takes, one thing seems certain—it is inevitable. As Donald Knuth (1974) has stated, "Perhaps the most significant discovery generated by the advent of computers will turn out to be that algorithms, as objects of study, are extraordinarily rich in interesting properties; and furthermore that an algorithmic point of view is a useful way to organize knowledge in general."

References

Burkoski, William, and Korotkin, Arthur. "Computing Activities in Secondary Education." *Educational Technology* (January 1976).

Chambers, J. A., and Bork, A. "Computer Assisted Learning in U.S. Secondary/Elementary Schools." Report No. 80–03. Fresno, Calif.: Center for Information Processing, California State University, 1980.

Knuth, D. E. "Computer Science and Its Relation to Mathematics." *American Mathematical Monthly* 81 (April 1974).

National Council of Teachers of Mathematics. *An Agenda for Action: Recommendations for School Mathematics for the 1980's.* Reston, Va.: NCTM, 1980.

National Council of Teachers of Mathematics. *Priorities in School Mathematics.* Reston, Va.: NCTM, 1981. Available from ERIC Documentation Reproduction Service, P.O. Box 190, Arlington, Virginia 22210.

---

[2]Stephen Rosowski, *Problems for Computer Solution* (Morristown, N.J.: Computing Press, 1980); E. R. Gage, *Problem-Solving with the Computer* (Newburyport, Mass.: ENTELEK Inc., 1969); E. R. Gage, *Fun and Games with the Computer* (Newburyport, Mass.: ENTELEK Inc., 1975); H. A. Maurer and M. R. Williams, *A Collection of Programming Problems and Techniques* (New York: Prentice-Hall, 1972); D. T. Piele, "Micros Go To School," *Creative Computing* 5 (September 1979): 132–134.

17. Computer Uses in the Social Studies

Donna M. Byrne

SOCIAL STUDIES INCLUDES A WIDE RANGE OF TOPICS THROUGHOUT SECONDARY education—foreign and domestic history, anthropology, world cultures, economics, geography, governmental structure and operations, and more. Computer-assisted learning can be applied to all of these areas.

Computer simulation programs allow students to conveniently experience situations they would not normally have in the real world. Simulations are recreated environments whose elements comprise a somewhat accurate representation or model of an external reality with which the players (students) interact in much the same way they would interact with the real world. Using simulations, students can experience the necessity to make decisions and are informed of the consequences without experiencing the negative results of misjudgments. These programs allow for student input and give immediate results of the situation at hand. By participating in simulations, students quickly realize the various effects that can result from a given situation that has ever-changing variables. Their interest is aroused and they are motivated to explore further by altering variables.

One of the most popular ways to use simulations is by teaching practical economics, such as family budgeting, investing, consumer decision making, and so forth. This type of lesson can be dealt with in game form using the computer and a program designed to simulate everyday life and its typical financial occurrences. Students may begin with some resources or none. They can plan for family expenses; make major life decisions in such areas as education, jobs, and careers; and simulate major purchases for homes, cars, and life insurance. These simulation games can also incorporate various unexpected financial disasters that might strike a family. The microcomputer is beneficial

124

because all mathematical calculations can be done more rapidly. The concept stressed here is the allocation of funds, not the mathematical operations. If the student does not make the appropriate decisions, the computer does. The next time, the situation can be altered somewhat and the student can try again.

Other topics that lend themselves to exploration by computer simulation programs include governmental economics and budget allocations, pollution development and control, and poverty levels and social welfare.

One of the greatest advantages of the computer is its ability to provide individualized instruction. Applicable programs are readily available from various software outlets (often listed in computer magazines) and prove to be informative to teachers and students alike.

Computer graphics is currently one of the fastest growing segments of the computer industry and finds excellent use in illustrating ideas that might complement lectures and readings. The primary reason for using graphics (computer or other) is to convey more complete information more rapidly. Our most important sense for learning might be considered sight because of the rich complexity of information that can be gathered visually. The brain perceives pictorial information in a mere glance—a process referred to as pre-attentive perception—but it must apprehend text or numerals in a more laborious, one-at-a-time fashion. During this "serial" operation, the processor of the brain must pay close attention and concentrate. In contrast, viewing pictures requires little effort and can be pleasurable.

Programs can easily be developed to construct graphs, maps, charts, and tables that graphically define concepts and ideas. "Computer graphics" can be used very effectively in the study of geography and economics. Maps can be drawn on the video display screen by using high-resolution graphics, adaptable to many microcomputers for moderate cost, or by using a sensorized graphics tablet.

Graphs can also be drawn to illustrate economic trends. Supply/demand curves, cost/revenue curves, and employment rates can be displayed on the computer screen demonstrating graphic results of an economic situation. And graphs can change as the economic situation changes and students can observe the results.

Many of the currently available microcomputers are quite capable of producing graphics. It is the programmer's responsibility to recognize when material can benefit from graphic representation. Graphics must support and enhance the written portion of a lesson.

Drill-and-practice programs assume that instruction in a concept has already been given. A general drill-and-practice paradigm has been developed incorporating principles of an effective associative learning episode and is applicable to a wide range of subject matter areas.

A game-like situation can also be incorporated into a drill-and-practice session. Games are often useful for maintaining a rapid learning pace and for adding to the student's affective involvement in the lesson, possibly increasing learning and retention. This type of approach is effective, for example, in memorizing facts. Several vendors are selling these programs now.

Computer-assisted learning is not intended to replace the teacher in the classroom. Its purpose, rather, is to exist as an educational tool used by both teacher and student. A combination of CAL and teacher interaction provides a better learning environment than a teacher can alone. Students using the CAL program work independently of other students and can progress as slowly or as quickly as they are able. In addition, students can also benefit from the computer's immediate response, which indicates the accuracy of answers while questions are still fresh in mind. Students learn to think more precisely since the computer is an extremely accurate machine. They learn by doing rather than by being told what to do.

References

Braun, Ludwig. *The Computer: Friend or Foe??* Program on Technology and Society, State University of New York, Stonybrook, 1976.

Classroom Computer News, Vol. 1, No. 6. Cambridge, Mass.: Lloyd R. Prentice Publishers, 1981.

Computer, Vols. 12, 13, Nos. 6, 10. San Jose, Calif.: IEEE Computer Society, 1979, 1980.

Creative Computing, Vol. 7, No. 3. Morristown, N.J.: Creative Computing, 1981.

Personal Computing, Vol. 5, No. 4. San Francisco, Calif.: Hayden Publishing Co., Inc., 1981.

Sanders, Donald H. *Computers in Society*. New York: McGraw-Hill Publishing Co., 1973.

The Computing Teacher, Vols. 7, 8, Nos. 5, 1. Eugene, Oreg.: University of Oregon, 1980, 1981.

18. Computers in the Teaching of English

Robert Shostak

MANY ENGLISH TEACHERS SEE THE COMPUTER ONLY AS A USEFUL TOOL for the mathematician, scientist, or the administrator. Consequently, they dismiss altogether the idea of using computers in their own work. Others see computers as a kind of robot-like creature, a view perpetuated by Hollywood science-fiction films; they simply do not take computers seriously. Still another group of English teachers—the tough old birds who have seen it all—nod their heads knowingly, while muttering (just loud enough for you to hear) something to the effect that it will not be too long before computers will be gathering dust in the closet alongside all the opaque projectors, television sets, phonograph players, and other once-heralded pieces of "modern" technology.

At one time or another I probably held some of these same views. Now, however, I do not think any English teacher can afford to subscribe to this kind of thinking. Because of the pervasiveness of the computer in every aspect of our public and private lives, we can no longer ignore its impact. More importantly, we cannot afford to ignore the potential it holds for education.

The use of technology and the need to understand its effects on society has not gone unnoticed in higher education either. Colleges and universities are looking for effective ways to integrate knowledge of technology with humanistic, ethical, and even theological considerations found in college curriculums. A unique program at Saint Louis University called "Man, Technology and Society" offers an English course called Madness in 20th Century Literature. As you might expect, the goal of this program and other similar programs is to demonstrate the importance of understanding the critical interplay of technology and the humanities in our rapidly changing society.

127

However, the decision to use computers in classrooms is not going to be made solely by English teachers. The integration of any new technology into existing systems is a difficult process even under the best conditions. It is no secret that public schools today are beset by more problems than they deserve.

The Need to Rethink the Concept of Teaching

Problem areas that professional educators are going to need to rethink carefully if computers are to be used effectively in our schools are those dealing with how children learn and the curriculum.

Seymour Papert, in his book, *Mindstorms: Children, Computers, and Powerful Ideas,* says that the teaching profession believes the way to increase learning is to improve teaching. This view, he says, simply creates ". . . an artificial and inefficient learning environment that society has been forced to invent because its informal environments fail in certain essential learning domains, such as writing or grammar or school math." Papert suggests educating young people to remove the artificiality from the learning environment and increase efficiency of learning based on the way a child learns to talk. He indicates that this complex learning task takes place in a natural environment without the benefit of "deliberate" or "organized teaching." Papert believes the computer can help create a more natural environment in which children will learn school knowledge as successfully and painlessly as they learned to talk.

If we adhere to the systematic "artificial," teacher-centered approach we rely on so heavily today, then the computer will become simply another instructional aide not much different from a tape recorder or overhead projector. However, if we begin to recast our thinking about the classroom environment and emphasize learning rather than teaching, then the computer will become the medium through which the student develops intellectual prowess and creates knowledge for himself.

Although most recent publicity has focused on the schools' inability to teach basic skills, the real weakness in the curriculum is in the area of problem solving. David Moursund, in his pamphlet *School Administrator's Introduction to Instructional Use of Computers,* presents an incisive analysis of the problem.

He accurately points out that most curriculum devoted to problem-solving focuses on carrying out a plan for the solution to a problem based on a formula or other recipe-like approach. Little time is spent on trying to understand the problem, formulate a solution, or interpret results. Moursund believes that computers can handle the formula portion of the problem-solving process better than people can. The computer can process information much faster and certainly with a higher degree of accuracy than humans. He suggests that our "overall curriculum needs to change, to reflect the role that calculators and computers best play in problem solving." Taking this direction will "decrease emphasis upon the routine and rote skills of carrying out a plan to solve a problem" and increase emphasis on the higher level skills of problem solving.

More specifically, if English teachers are not going to be able to use the computer to help students develop higher order thinking skills, they are going to reject its use in the classroom. English teachers want students to develop their skills in analysis, synthesis, and evaluation. These are the critical skills required for competency in the areas of literature, language, and communications.

In addition to the need to recast their thinking about the nature of curriculum and the way students learn, English teachers must consider their own professional development. Two pieces of reality that English teachers face at this time are lack of knowledge about computers and the rapid rate at which the technology is advancing. The solution to the first problem is education. As quickly as possible, English teachers should and must demand effective computer literacy training. With a sound understanding of how the computer functions and what it is capable of doing as a learning tool, teachers can then begin to conceive better the possibilities inherent in using computers in the English classroom.

The solution to the second problem is not as simple. Computer technology is advancing at such a rapid rate that I sometimes feel that if I don't step out of the way it will run right over me. What could happen is that, as teachers, we might find ourselves at the mercy of those who control the technology but do not necessarily understand what is really important in the teaching of English.

As professionals, then, English teachers will have to play a major role in establishing guidelines for development of computer courseware for the language arts. More specifically, English teachers will have to help define the curriculum content and objectives that are taught best by computers. They will have to suggest innovative uses of this new technology and identify appropriate areas of research. Finally, English teachers will have to assume a major part of the responsibility for making other English teachers aware of how computers can be used effectively in the classroom.

Computer Applications in English Classes

The use of computers in the classroom by English teachers is presently very limited. It is limited both by the lack of equipment and availability of good computer courseware. Teachers fortunate enough to have computers are using them for the most part as teacher aides. For example, packaged programs produced by well-known publishers of educational materials and some recent newcomers are being used to teach spelling, punctuation, parts of speech, and vocabulary.

Other computer programs provide drill-and-practice exercises in these curriculum areas so that students may develop and extend their skill. A distinct advantage of using the computer in this way is that it provides some students with truly individualized instruction and an accurate up-to-the-minute record of their progress while freeing the teacher to provide other students with learning opportunities that require close teacher/student interaction.

A number of imaginative computer uses helps students better understand and appreciate poetry. Using simple programs to generate lines of poetry in specifically structured patterns, such as a haiku, some English teachers have had great success in teaching about the creative process. Students who understand how the computer generates poems are quickly inspired to create their own poetry using the computer program as a guide. The heuristic nature of this activity brings students face to face with problems all authors experience in creative writing. They must pay careful attention to planning, diction, spelling, punctuation, and grammar. More importantly, they are quickly and easily able to share each other's work to engage in critical exchanges that lead to a greater understanding of and deeper appreciation for poetry and the creative process.

Some teachers have found that the computer's ability to function as a word processor is extremely helpful in teaching composition. This capability allows students to compose on the computer's keyboard; save their work so that it may be recalled at a future time; edit (at the touch of a key) every aspect of what has been written, including the shifting of sentences and paragraphs from one location to another; and print out a finished product without having to be concerned about spacing, pagination, headings, or margins. In other words, revision, so necessary in the process of learning how to write well yet so distasteful to students, can be so simplified by the word processing power of the computer that students who have tried it actually enjoy it.

Another innovative application involves computer adventure games similar to Dungeons and Dragons in teaching certain aspects of literature. For example, students find it very easy to understand the literary elements of plot development and characterization once they understand how an adventure game employs similar techniques in its format. The adventure game is also a great motivational tool for developing students' creative thinking powers. It makes them aware of their creative ability—a rich but untapped resource in many students—and, more importantly, provides an area for students to produce new ideas and new creations of their own.

Lastly, there is the powerful management capability of the computer, which English teachers are finding especially helpful in their classrooms. Many teachers no longer need to be concerned with the clerical function associated with administering, scoring, and recording test results. The computer as a grade book is accurate, efficient, and remarkably swift in calculating final grades and providing the teacher with complete printouts of class assignments, student rankings, and a variety of statistical information valuable for instructional decision making.

Although many educators are not yet aware, we are, without a doubt, in the midst of a technological revolution that is already having its effect on a number of English classrooms around the country. The National Council of Teachers of English, anticipating rapid changes, has appointed a standing committee on instructional technology to begin developing a specific plan to help English teachers integrate technology into existing English programs.

If educators fail to meet the needs of society as it moves inexorably into the age of advanced technology, they may find themselves in the same shaky position the American car industry finds itself today. The failure of Detroit to make the successful transition from the technology of electro/mechanical production to the technology of the computer has cost them the number one position in auto manufacturing throughout the world and a corresponding loss of billions of dollars. American car manufacturers may recover from this setback. The education establishment may not get a second chance.

References

Toffler, Alvin. *The Third Wave*. New York: William Morrow and Co., 1980.

Papert, Seymour. *Mindstorms: Children, Computers, and Powerful Ideas*. New York: Basic Books, 1980.

19. Computer Uses in Business Education

Eugene J. Muscat and Paul Lorton, Jr.

FOR BUSINESS EDUCATORS, THE CHALLENGE POSED BY COMPUTERS CENTERS ON providing students with experiences that will enable them to deal with computers in their work almost as soon as they leave the classroom.

This is no small task. Most business educators received their training before computers were in widespread use in business and industry. Even recent graduates in business education are amazed by the wide applications the computer has found outside the classroom. Not only do many business teachers have some catching up to do, nearly all will have to hustle in order to keep up with this rapidly developing technology.

Problems Facing Business Education

There are two types of problems facing business education: (1) acquiring resources, and (2) enhancing the curriculum. Both exist because society itself is in transition between a noncomputerized and a computerized technology. The industrial revolution took generations. It is unlikely that computerization will take longer than a few years. Both problems begin at the same source—convincing the resource allocators that business education needs computer resources as much as or more than science, math, and other "college prep" departments. In most cases, the business community realizes this need and can provide support—by contributing resources.

Acquiring resources in times of reduced budgets is a considerable problem. The need is clear and the equipment is decreasing in price; yet it is never easy to spend money on equipment when teachers are being asked to make do with less. The solution, which we will discuss in detail later, involves broad-based planning as well as making equipment available on a schoolwide basis in "neutral territory."

The second major problem is in enhancing the curriculum to use computers where appropriate for the student's educational experience. There are two contributing difficulties here: (1) materials are scarce, and (2) teachers are ill-prepared. Again, the solution involves education. Administrators must allow business educators together with curriculum workers release time to revise the curriculum, locate or develop new materials, and promote faculty computer literacy.

As in all curricular areas, the computer has been used in a wide variety of ways in business education, but not extensively. Fifty years after Herman Holerith's punched card data processing, teaching with and about unit record equipment was still considered a modern innovation in business education classes. Less than 50 years after the first digital computer, teaching with and about computers is still considered an innovation and often a luxury. Regardless of this slow start, the move is on to employ the computer as the means, manager, and object of instruction.

The Computer as a Means of Instruction

The term "computer-assisted instruction" describes an activity whereby the computer is used as the "means" of problem solving, drill and practice, simulation, or tutorial experience. Several applications— some of which have been mentioned in other chapters—can be implemented easily by local staff and provide valuable service to business education programs.

Drill and Practice

Spelling. Business education courses spend an extensive amount of instructional time on spelling. Computer programs easily provide the drill-and-practice aspect of spelling review, permit students to select individualized spelling lists, and provide a competency record. Spelling programs of this type are flexible and can accommodate technical terms used for medical and legal courses.

Vocabulary review. Many students require fundamental review of vocabulary, particularly business terminology, prior to subject matter instruction. The computer can be particularly useful in this case, since it can be assigned only to those students who have a diagnosed vocabulary weakness.

Simulation

Brief form review. Some applications make partial use of the simulation capabilities of the computer. Students can use a computer program that provides individualized reinforcement of shorthand brief forms they encounter in the classroom. This is particularly useful on computers having a timing function, which permits the student to select a time interval between the presentation of shorthand brief forms. As the computer presents words chosen randomly from the shorthand brief list, students copy the brief form, gaining maximum practice on dictation drills. When a printing terminal is used, the instructor can assign such drills for homework, requesting that students copy the forms on the computer print-out terminal during drill and practice. The computer can compute the words per minute based on the length of the drill and the number of brief forms completed.

Making change. The simulation capabilities of the computer are particularly helpful in basic skills training. A popular program, for example, generates random transactions for students in a simulated cashier's position. The student must return the correct change in accordance with rules introduced by the instructor (and the computer). Students discover that only 100 percent competency is acceptable in this type of job simulation.

Tutorial

Computer programming instruction. The computer can be used to introduce topics where a full course of instruction is not possible. Tutorial lessons on the computer introduce the topic, encourage the student to investigate concepts, and provide drill-and-practice follow-up. This technique is particularly useful to teachers who want to meet the needs of a limited number of students on an advanced topic (accounting, business law, and so forth).

A major instructional advantage of the computer is that it introduces students to a common tool in the office of the future and emphasizes the importance of keyboarding skills. Computer-assisted drills provide the teacher with a round-the-clock paraprofessional aide that allows students to review before school, after school, during free periods, or when released from regular classroom instruction. It is not uncommon for students to voluntarily spend hours on outside review apart from required classroom instruction.

The Computer as Manager of Instruction

While less compelling than CAI, computer-managed instruction (CMI) is much more appealing to many teachers and most administrators. One small computer, grading tests or tracking attendance, can have a greater impact on school organization than a large computer giving math lessons to a few students every day. CMI can be used with a single computer system equipped with a scanner/reader. A CMI application typically includes:

1. Student assessment (placement tests)
2. Primary remedial assignments
3. Post-assessment testing
4. Alternate remedial assignments
5. Certification

For example, a CMI business English program could "certify" students in spelling, punctuation, grammar, and so on. Steps 2, 3, and 4 often need to be repeated several times before certification is achieved. An output printer is necessary for CMI so that remedial assignments can be printed and distributed to students (steps 2 and 4). A hidden value of this type of system is that advanced classes consisting of only a few students can monitor their own results by testing and retesting themselves or working from individualized education plans (IEP) when the teacher cannot provide help immediately.

Accounting Applications

Computers are rapidly becoming the tool of the accountant. Accounting curricula can make effective use of computer systems as the means of instruction and the object of instruction. Reinforcement of basic accounting concepts can be accomplished with the use of course author languages (CAL). These lesson-building tools can rapidly produce "interactive" sequences to help students understand troublesome concepts (balancing accounts, depreciation, closing entries, and so on). CAL lessons are ideal for remediation outside of large-group instruction. Lessons are usually tutorial in nature, designed by the instructor to reinforce crucial learning concepts. Vocational preparation demands that accounting students understand the role of computers in the storage, calculation, and retrieval of financial data. This can be accomplished by simulation of standard office operations using General Ledger, Accounts Receivable/Payable or Payroll software. With widespread microcomputer use in small businesses there is a broad range of financial application software available for classroom use.

Keyboarding

Keyboarding curriculum is the contemporary evolution of a personal typing course conducted by the business education department. With large numbers of computer literate students on today's campuses the appeal of a keyboarding course seems timely. Microcomputers are ideal for keyboard training since they can demand 100 percent accuracy during timed drills.

CAI keyboarding courseware usually displays a sample text asking the student to re-enter each character. Errors are immediately identified, specific deficiencies diagnosed, and directions given to students to work on weaknesses. While diagnosis should take place at computer terminals, remediation can be performed at typewriters. Certification should be accomplished via computer terminal to alleviate teacher recordkeeping.

Data Processing

The use of computer equipment in data processing instruction parallels that of accounting—The computer is used during instruction as both the object and the means of instruction. Computer operations, data entry, word processing and computer support training rely heavily on "hands-on" equipment demonstrations, often accomplished with heavy use of CAI courseware. Most microcomputer companies offer CAI programming lessons to introduce fundamental programming concepts. Using the concept of "the medium is the message" many data processing students' first experience with computers is in programming tutorial lessons. Vocational preparation and certification requires a maximum of student-equipment contact. This can be accomplished on an individualized basis and merged with the operations of the school's computer center.

Word Processing

The hardware described above can and should be adapted to the teaching of word processing skills. Students with appropriate keyboarding and English proficiencies can be effectively trained to perform the production jobs that support the business education department. Data entry, which concentrates on numeric keyboarding, can be carried out in a manner similar to word processing. The students involved, however, may not require equivalent language skills.

Computer Programming

The issue of computer programming instruction is complex. Increased computer literacy in America will soon make programming instruction mandatory in any business education department. The choice of hardware and software needs to be locally adapted to the needs of business and industry. Fortunately, publishers have provided a wealth of materials to make instruction in any language possible on an individualized basis. Most computer manufacturers offer tutorial (CAI) courseware that teaches the fundamentals of several computer languages.

Recommendations

What is should point the way to what should be. The recommendations that follow are strategies for future success. They are based on the premise that enrollments and community support are not desirable, but essential.

1. *Establish five-year planning for computer use.* While this should be a districtwide effort, it can begin in your business education department with the following steps:

a. Discuss what is.
b. Develop a "wish list."
c. Gather data and visit sites of successful programs.
d. Adopt standards for hardware and software.
e. Expand on success; learn from failure.
f. Publicize your activities.
g. Cooperate with the local educational community—promote "neutral territory" for computer use.

2. *Fight for business education-based computer literacy instruction.* Why business education? BE departments are appropriate for equipment. They have power, space, equipment, and experience that other departments do not. BE is best qualified to teach keyboarding, an essential computer literacy skill. Computer literacy should include consumer applications, which is a BE discipline. Finally, computer literacy opens students' eyes to prevocational and vocational interests, which are best met in a well-equipped BE department.

3. *Develop and operate a student-run computer center.* Even if you only have a single piece of equipment, use it for production data processing. Your department and school is a functioning business system. Student staff are more than equal to performing the following EDP operations:

a. Word processing
b. Test scoring
c. Questionnaire evaluation
d. Attendance accounting
e. Budget reporting
f. Inventory control

In this way, you can make maximum use of district and federal funding as well as provide needed school services. Business education has a history of providing school services. This activity should accelerate with the introduction of high technology equipment.

4. *Strengthen business and industry involvement.* As we visit school districts, we often see a struggle for computer leadership among the business, math, and science departments. It is regrettable that such confusion exists. With the advent of five-year planning committees, the issues should be resolved. It is important, however, that districts seek active participation of business and industry in this process. The tax burden for schools weighs heavily on local businesses. Even more pressing is their need for computer literate graduates. No curriculum planning should take place without widespread business and industry involvement.

20. Computer Uses in The Arts and Humanities

Beverly J. Jones

Instruction in Fundamentals

Within each of the arts students receive instruction in certain fundamental concepts and skills. The ability to recognize basic structural components and perform simple tasks using these components is usually included in instructional goals. To affect these goals, several CAI programs have been created and tested in visual arts, music, and the humanities.

Visual Arts

The identification and manipulation of the components of visual design is fundamental to an understanding of the visual arts, as is a conceptual grasp of the varieties of visual combinations and interpretations these components may evoke. Among those active in the study of computer uses in teaching visual arts fundamentals is the computer research group at the Ohio State University. Recently this group has incorporated the techniques of McFee and Degge for teaching fundamentals of perspective and the depiction of three dimensions on a flat surface in a CAI program for elementary school students. At the University of Delaware, Raymond Nichols has developed a number of lessons in art fundamentals for the PLATO system. These include "Composition Using Grey Scale Tones," "Design Aesthetics and Creation," and "Letter Spacing," among others, which stress the computer as a media tool rather than as an instructional device for basic concepts. According to Nichols, the "Unit Design" program provides a solution

---

Earlier versions of this chapter appeared in the Association for Computing Machinery *Preliminary Report* (April 1980) and *The Computing Teacher* 9 (November 1980).

to four distinct problems that affect beginning visual design students:

1. Students' limited visual presentation of ideas resulting from their level of basic technical skills.

2. Students' visual presentations based not on their aesthetic tastes, but on expediency—it is easier to change one's taste than to change the design.

3. Teachers' difficulty in evaluating students' work. Students' varying mix of technical and conceptual skills complicate separating them for discussion or criticism.

4. Teachers' difficulty in effectively criticising students' work. The experiences and tastes instructors bring to evaluations are not the same ones students use in interpreting evaluations.

Nichols' program alleviates these problems by reducing the technical skills required for executing a design, and provides all students with the same range of choices for implementing a design with equal ease. The instructor's evaluation need not consider the manner in which the design was created, but only the design's compositional success. Other University of Delaware PLATO programs include typography, basic illustration, advertising design, and portfolio preparation.

Aaron Marcus at the University of California at Berkeley and Kenneth Knowlton at Bell Labs have developed courses that use the computer as a graphic tool for developing visual concepts and graphic design. These courses present a promising approach to teaching not only art fundamentals, but the programming skills necessary for designing on a computer graphics system. Knowlton has developed a computer language called EXPLOR for teaching computer graphics and computer art. A smaller version of this language, MINI-EXPLOR, will run on minicomputers and requires only 8 to 16K of core memory storage. Courses like these are useful to instructors who want to use computers in creating CAI materials in the visual arts.

Music

Programs for teaching music fundamentals to various age groups have been developed at a number of facilities, including Stanford University and the University of Delaware where programmers have developed systems for instruction and research in ear training. Drill-and-practice and game simulation strategies are used to teach pitch and interval recognition, dictation of melody, chords, harmony, and rhythm. Exercises to assist the student in sight reading and instrumental methods have also been developed. Studies conducted on groups of students using these instructional programs indicate that CAI is as effective or more effective than conventional instruction. Using a system developed at the University of Delaware called GUIDO, instructors can study individual differences among students as well as group tendencies.

Humanities

Within the humanities is a variety of approaches to teaching fundamentals. Jordan and others (1976), in an index of community college English lessons, list CAI units on "capitalization, composition, editing, grammar, poetry, punctuation, research, spelling, usage, vocabulary, and miscellaneous," which reflect a concern with the basic structural elements of language and the concepts for combining them. Language instructors in French, German, Spanish, Latin, and ancient Greek are also using computers to teach vocabulary, grammar, and translation skills.

At a higher level of difficulty, but still essential to a fundamental understanding of humanities, are programs that help students identify key ideas in their reading of literature and philosophy. The skills necessary to understand the basics of language—spelling, vocabulary, grammar, the structure of literary forms, and the more complex skills of understanding and interpreting these forms—have all been taught using CAI.

Implications

It appears that many of the repetitive aspects of teaching fundamentals are capably handled by computer-assisted instruction. This gives students greater control over their learning process in several ways. They may repeat a task as many times as necessary to achieve success without interrupting the instructor or slowing other students. The level of material presented may also be varied with greater ease than in a conventional classroom, resulting in greater instructional flexibility.

Even so, using the computer in an instructional mode that dictates the range of student choices causes some educators to question its appropriateness. Certainly if this were the only instruction available it would be questionable. However, when several alternative programs are available and the instructor is also present, these programs contribute to the quality of instruction. The instructor, freed from continual repetition, can concentrate on helping individual students use their knowledge and skills to interact with CAI lessons. The extent to which this type of instruction is appropriate is a question that curriculum developers need to consider. Too great a use of drill-and-practice materials will lead to the charge that the computer is being used to program students and limit their choices and concepts.

Composing With the Computer

Visual artists, musicians, dancers, and a few poets have experimented with the computer as a device for creating artistic forms. Usually they attempt to emulate traditional forms, using the computer as a designing or composing device. However, some are exploring the unique qualities of the computer as a media device.

Visual Arts

Numerous conventional art processes have been radically altered by computers—most notably, graphic design, industrial design, advertising art, and film animation. Many visual images that we see today are products of computers used as a design tool. Those who design and execute woven textiles also frequently rely on computer assistance for some phase of their work. Artists working in such areas as sculpture, printmaking, drawing, and painting are experimenting with the computer as an aid to design or execution of their work. The speed with which designs can be created, manipulated, and stored in a computer graphics system contributes to its appeal to artists.

The line between the arts is blurred by individuals who use the computer to create unique instruments. Bonacic and Ihnowitz, for instance, have created computer-controlled sculptures that are responsive to changes in environment, such as alteration in light, sound, and movement. Other artists are trying to create responsive environments that effect shape, color, lighting, air movement, and temperature in response to a variety of input from the artist.

Music

Computer instruments for composing and performing music range from small hand-held musical calculators to the elaborate facilities of Stanford's Center for Computer Research in Music and Acoustics. Computers have been used for controlling or emulating traditional and electronic instruments as well as serving as digital musical instruments or controlling unique musician-built devices. A January 1980 report from the Center for Research in Music and Acoustics states: "As a musical instrument the computer system is possibly the most flexible of all instruments. To speak of it as a conventional music instrument, however, is somewhat misleading because the system is capable of simultaneously producing a large number of independent voices having arbitrary timbral characteristics."

Studies conducted at the Center, which examined the way sounds are made, led to the creation of a computer controlled music synthesizer that emulates sounds made by conventional instruments. Thus a person using the computer controlled synthesizer could hear a composition played by a simulated violin, clarinet, oboe, and cello; by a single instrument; or by a simulated full orchestra. The space in which the sounds are played may be varied also. Several universities have facilities that allow students to try out these capabilities.

Lief Brush at the University of Iowa has created unconventional "instruments" that sometimes blur the distinctions among musical instrument, sculpture, and conceptual performance piece. An example of his work is the Riverharp structure. The use of electronics and computer control is essential to the success of experimental instruments of this type.

Finally, David Ashton reports the development of a project using a computer controlled organ in conjunction with a graphics scope. Children aged four to 12, as well as adults, have used the equipment to compose music and to manipulate compositions.

Humanities

Fewer projects using the computer as a compositional device have been conducted in the humanities than in visual art or music. Early work using computers for poetic composition made extensive use of random selection from a set of programmed alternatives. Programs of this sort are frequently used in elementary schools to compose haiku or cinquain. Students create a series of alternatives for each section of the poetic form, then use the computer to compose alternative poems using the input in various combinations.

More recent work involves the use of programs for stylistic analysis. These make it possible to compose within stylistic rules controlled by the programmer rather than by random selection. Some poets and artists who are interested in the visual qualities of poems are constructing concrete poems using the computer as a graphic designing tool. The results of these experiments blur the distinction between the literary and visual arts. Programs intended primarily for computer graphics—such as those that select and generate symbols and typographical forms, then alter their size, slant, or location—are suited to the development of concrete poetry.

Implications

Since much of the current curriculum focus in both music and visual arts is in performance and production, curriculum developers need to consider the potential for change that these projects offer. They raise several questions. For example, in the work of avant-garde artists, musicians, and poets, there is a blurring between the arts. Is this appropriate to introduce in an early phase of a child's education? Also a student may, with the aid of computer controlled synthesizers, listen to a full orchestral rendition of a simple theme just composed—yet remain ignorant of the years it takes a human being to learn to perform on a single instrument or to conduct an orchestra. Similarly, a student who has little knowledge of the craft of weaving can see examples of a newly designed woven tapestry displayed on a color television. In short, the technical aspects of the arts, which absorb much time and are a primary source of learning, would be subordinated to the conceptual aspects of the same tasks. The number of experiments students can attempt in the same period of time could be vastly increased. Certainly this could affect the design of the scope and sequence of a proposed curriculum using computer-assisted composition.

The computer as a controller of other mechanical and electronic devices is a major source of inspiration for a number of contemporary artists as well as science instructors. For example, Seymour Papert has been allowing children to experiment with the interface of various devices with the computer, including a plotting (drawing) unit, music boxes, lights, and electric motors. Students who have access to a laboratory situation of this type have a much greater chance of understanding artists' work as well as greater opportunities to explore concepts of industrial automation.

Analysis, Criticism, and Instruction

Researchers in the arts and humanities are using computer programs that store and analyze large quantities of information. The potential this has for students to analyze artistic forms and their own preferences and for teachers to analyze their instructional performance is only beginning to be explored.

Visual Arts

Some studies have attempted to analyze and simulate artistic style in the visual arts. Nolls and Nake conducted an experiment involving simulation and preference testing of the work of Piet Mondrian. Nake attempted to simulate the artistic styles of Paul Klee and Hans Hartung.

Although less developed, these experiments may be compared with the simulations of Bach or Shakespeare.

The work of Linehan (1980), who explored computer-assisted analysis of visual preferences, has great potential for developing teaching models of art criticism that allow students to explore their own critical judgments and compare them to others.

Music

Ashton (1973) designed an educational environment with a computer-controlled organ that displays musical information in a graphic form for use by elementary school children. This allows them to see a graphic visual representation of parts of a musical score. Children may redraw parts of the score and hear the effect of changes on the sound of the music represented by the line drawing. The interaction of students with the system can be recorded for later analysis of instructional effectiveness.

Researchers who have analyzed music of various periods and composers to understand structural differences have simulated those styles. Students who have access to information gained from these stylistic analyses could experiment by composing within structural limits or by selectively departing from them. From individualized experimentation like this, an understanding of musical structure and style could emerge that would be difficult to achieve using other instructional methods.

Humanities

Stylistic studies in the humanities are revealing structural relationships within an author's work. This is used by researchers to attribute authorship to questioned passages. By studying the factors revealed in these statistical measures, such as richness of vocabulary and interesting word patterns, students can derive a deeper understanding of the stylistic characteristics differentiating authors and periods in literature.

A course developed by B. J. Jones provides a model for assisting students in developing skills in analysis and criticism. Using CAI in a religious studies course at California State College, Jones teaches a theory of biblical authorship, provides practice in literary criticism, and elicits judgments about the theory. These exercises help students develop skills of interpretation and analysis, and in making and defending critical judgments.

Another course at Vassar teaches students to use the computer as an analytical tool to discover patterns in literature and to test possible interpretations of these patterns. Students have analyzed such diverse data as the language of Milton's *Paradise Lost* and the Watergate testimony.

Implications

Common among the analytical programs described for the arts and humanities is the process of finding reliable patterns in data, then testing their possible interpretations or limits. This fosters an unusual problem-solving approach to the subject matter of the arts and humanities. It is up to curriculum developers to determine whether this would provide a valuable adjunct to the current curriculum.

Further Implications and Recommendations

Precollege art educators should begin to determine the directions their use of computers will take in the future. As the availability of small personal computers in elementary and secondary schools increases, their use by all instructors will increase. Awareness of projects that employ these devices and appropriate peripherals in successful instructional settings is essential to the development of good precollege programs. By reading studies and obtaining hands-on experience with a variety of hardware configurations and software systems, precollege arts instructors will develop their abilities to purchase appropriate hardware and software for classrooms. Without these experiences, their ability to weigh the benefits and limitations of specific types of CAI, composition, and critical analysis would be severely diminished.

As instructors become more knowledgeable, they will need to address questions of selectivity and curricular suitability. They will have to consider the computer's abilities to store and search large bodies of information; to repeat a single task with slight variations without tiring; to provide many branches within instructional, compositional, or analytical programs; to keep accurate records of student interactions; to provide dramatic examples of sound and graphics in conjunction with essentially static lessons; and to provide students with the opportunity to experience in a direct way links between the arts and between the arts and sciences.

This latter computer capability is a significant factor in the unification of subject matter experiences in precollege education. Instructional sequences that allow students to program or experiment with computer hardware, perhaps creating unique output devices like those described in this article, create meaningful links between the arts and sciences within the student's immediate experience. Instructors may also consider creating projects that encourage overlap in instruction between physics and the arts as students study video or musical synthesis. Opportunities to visit research facilities such as Stanford's Center for Computer Research in Music and Acoustics or the electronic studios in the Chicago Art Institute would be beneficial to either arts or science instruction in a secondary school.

Also bearing potential for suggesting interdisciplinary curricular directions is Marcus' (1979) graphic communication project, "Visualizing Global Interdependencies." In this project, data from the social sciences and physical sciences are combined to show their global human significance using a dramatic graphic treatment. Students working on a similar type of project would rapidly become aware of the interrelationships among the isolated facts they learn in various classes.

Finally, a case study approach examining the accomplishments of individuals working in an interdisciplinary manner using computers, particularly those incorporating their interests in both the arts and sciences, would seem valuable. As the projects, experiences, and attitudes of these individuals are examined, more ideas will emerge to enrich our concept of computer uses in the classroom.

References

Allvin, R. L. "Computer-Assisted Music Instruction: A Look at the Potential." *Journal of Research in Music Education* 19 (1971): 131–143.

Alfonso, S.; Appleton, J. H.; and Jones, C. A. "A Special Purpose Digital System for the Instruction, Composition and Performance of Music." Proceedings of the Sixth Conference on Computers in the Undergraduate Curriculum, 1975.

Ashton, D. M. "Design of an Educational Environment with a Computer-Controlled Organ." Intermountain Regional Medical Program, Salt Lake City, Utah, 1973.

Brush, L. "Terrain Instrument/Riverharps Affiliate." *Numus West* 2 (1975): 47–50.

Chowning, J. M.; Grey, J. M.; Moorer, J. A.; Rush, L.; and Smith, L. C. "Report from Center for Computer Research in Music and Acoustics." Stanford University, January 1980.

Della-Piana, G. M. "The Development of a Model for the Systematic Teaching of the Writing of Poetry. Final Report." Salt Lake City, Utah: Utah University, Salt Lake City Bureau of Educational Research, August 1971.

Diehl, N. C., and Siegler, R. H. "Evaluation of a CAI Program in Articulation, Phrasing, and Rhythm for Intermediate Instrumentalists." *Council for Research in Music Education* 31 (1973): 1–11.

Eddings, J. M. "Random Access Audio in Computer Assisted Music Instruction." *Journal of Computer Based Instruction* 5 (1978): 22–29.

Ettinger, L. F. "Portrait of a Secondary Teacher." *The Computing Teacher* 9 (October 1981): 49–50.

Ettinger, L. F., and Jones, B. J. "Portrait of a High School Student." *The Computing Teacher* 9 (November 1981): 55–57.

Gilbert, B. "The Computerized Artist, A Graphics Unit for Artists Who Aren't Programmers." *Interface Age* (December 1979).

Heller, J. J., and others. "Graphic Representation of Musical Concepts: A Computer Assisted Instructional System. Final Report." Storrs: Connecticut University, 1971.

Henkels, R. M., Jr., and Egea, E. R. "Using a Computer-Generated Concordance to Analyze and Document Stylistic Devices in Robert Pinget's Fable." *Computer and Humanities* 11 (1977): 325–328.

Hofstetter, F. T. "Fourth Summative Report of the Delaware PLATO Report." Newark: University of Delaware, 1979.

Hofstetter, F. T. "Instructional Design and Curricular Impact of Computer Based Music Education." *Educational Technology* 18 (1978): 50–53.

Hofstetter, F. T. "GUIDO: An Interactive Computer-Based System for Improvement of Instruction and Research in Ear-Training." *Journal of Computer Based Instruction* 1 (1975): 100–106.

Jones, B. J. "Computer Applications in the Arts and Humanities." *The Computing Teacher* 8 (1980–81): 22–30.

Jones, B. J. "Instructional Potential of the Computer in Visual Arts Education, ES3 Report." February 1980.

Jones, B. J. "ACM Elementary and Secondary Schools Subcommittee, Preliminary Report." April 1980.

Jones, B. J. "Religious Studies as a Test Case for Computer Assisted Instruction in the Humanities." Conference in Computers in the Undergraduate Curricula, Claremont, California, June 1973.

Jones, M. J. "Computer Assisted Instruction in Music: A Survey with Attendant Recommendations." Doctoral dissertation, Northwestern University, 1975.

Jordan, P., and others. *Community College English Lesson Index*. Urbana, Ill.: Illinois University, Computer Based Education Laboratory, 1976.

Lefkoff, G. "Computers and the Study of Musical Style." *Computer Applications in Music*, West Virginia Library (1967): 43–61.

Linehan, T. E. "A Computer Mediated Model for Visual Preference Research with Implications for the Teaching of Art Criticism." Doctoral dissertation, Ohio State University, 1980.

Malina, F. J., ed. *Visual Art, Mathematics, and Computers*. Pergamon Press, 1979.

Marcus, A. "New Ways to View World Problems." *East West Perspective* 1 (1979): 15–22.

Maslow, A. H. *The Farther Reaches of Human Nature*. New York: The Viking Press, 1971.

Moorer, J. A., and Gray, J. "Lexicon of Analyzed Tones: Part 1—A Violin Tone." *Computer Music Journal* 1 (1977): 39–45.

Moorer, J. A., and Gray J. "Lexicon of Analyzed Tones: Part 2—Clarinet and Oboe Tones." *Computer Music Journal* 1 (1977): 12–29.

Moorer, J. A., and Gray, J. "Lexicon of Analyzed Tones: Part 3—The Trumpet." *Computer Music Journal* 2 (1978): 23–31.

Noll, A. M. *Human or Machine: A Subjective Comparison of Piet Mondrian's Composition with Lines (1917) and a Computer Generated Picture*. Baltimore: Penguin Books, 1969.

Paisley, W. J. "Identifying the Unknown Communicator in Painting, Literature, and Music: The Significance of Minor Encoding Habits." *Journal of Communications* 14 (1964): 219–237.

Paisley, W. J. "The Museum Computer and the Analysis of Artistic Content." Conference on Computers and Thier Potential Applications in Museums, 1968.

Papert, S., and Solomon, C. "Twenty Things To Do With a Computer." *Artificial Intelligence Memo No. 248*. Cambridge: Massachusetts Institute of Technology.

Peters, G. D., and Eddings, J. M. "Research: A Selected Bibliography." *Journal of Computer Based Instruction* 5 (1978): 41–44.

Ray, D., and Killam, R. M. "Melodic Perception Development and Measurement Through CAI." Proceedings of NECC 1979 National Educational Computing Conference, Iowa City, 1979.

Vaughn, A. C., Jr. "A Study of the Contrast Between Computer-Assisted Instruction and the Traditional Teacher/Learner Method of Instruction in Basic Musicianship." Doctoral dissertation, Oregon State University, 1977.

21. Computers in Music Education: The GUIDO System

Fred T. Hofstetter

THE MICRO GUIDO EAR-TRAINING SYSTEM IS AN EXAMPLE of computer-based music instruction. With complete programming in intervals, melodies, chords, harmonies, and rhythms, GUIDO uses high-resolution graphics, touch input, and a fully programmable sound synthesizer to provide a rich music learning environment. A comprehensive set of instructor options allows teachers to adjust the GUIDO system to their own needs, and keep records on student progress in the curriculum. A careful process of research and evaluation (see bibliography) has documented the effectiveness of the system, and recent advances in microelectronics now make it available at an affordable price.

Guido D'Arezzo was the eleventh century monk who invented the staff and the solfeggio syllables *do, re, mi, fa, sol,* and *la.* Since he was the first real music educator, the system has been named after him, using his first name as an acronym for Graded Units for Interactive Dictation Operations. Each GUIDO program is divided into units of instruction that are graded as to their levels of difficulty. The programs are highly interactive, with the students participating in a constant dialogue with the GUIDO system. Each GUIDO unit consists of a set of drill-and-practice dictation exercises. Dictation is the primary means of measuring student progress in aural skills; if a student can listen to a musical example and write it down, then surely the student has heard it properly.

Development of the GUIDO system began at the University of Delaware in 1974. Programs are written, tested with students, and revised on the Delaware PLATO® System, and then down-line loaded on floppy disks to run in a low-cost format on micro PLATO stations.

The Micro GUIDO Music Learning Station

The micro GUIDO learning station consists of a micro PLATO display, a University of Delaware sound synthesizer, a set of earphones through which the student listens to the music, and a floppy disk drive. Since the PLATO screen is touch-sensitive, the student can interact with GUIDO lessons by simply touching musical symbols drawn on the screen. The resulting interaction is immediate and highly stimulating, and the use of touch input makes it possible for the student to work with symbols that would be much too complex to enter by means of an ordinary computer keyset. The high-resolution graphics of the micro PLATO screen make it possible for a lot of musical information to be displayed at once, as will be seen in the following discussion of the five GUIDO programs.

Intervals

Figure 1 shows a sample display from the intervals program.[1] At the top are two rows of boxes that contain the names of musical intervals. GUIDO plays one of the intervals, and the students respond by touching the box that contains the interval they think they played. GUIDO keeps score, informing the students of how many intervals they have answered correctly, and how many more they need to do before they pass the unit they are in. All five of the GUIDO programs use this goal-oriented, competency-based approach that ensures students know the material at one level before proceeding on to the next.

Underneath the interval names are three columns of control boxes which are used to control the way in which dictation is given. The teacher can pre-set them for students or allow students to set them at will. The first column of boxes allows for the intervals to be played as harmonic, melodic up, melodic down, or melodic intervals up and down. The second column gives the option of being able to fix the top or bottom notes of the interval, or to have them selected at random. In the third column of boxes the student can select compound or simple intervals, have an interval played again, or change the length of time the intervals last. Finally there is a keyboard at the bottom of the screen. The student uses this keyboard to indicate top and bottom notes for intervals when using the "fix top" and "fix bottom" control boxes.

---

[1]All sample displays from the GUIDO programs presented here are copyrighted by the University of Delaware.

Figure 1
Sample display from the GUIDO Intervals Program

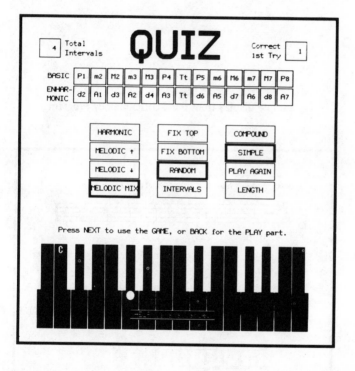

Melodies

Figure 2 shows a sample from the melody program. GUIDO plays a melody for the student, and then asks the student to enter the melody by touching the correct pitches on the display. As the student touches the correct pitches, GUIDO writes them on the staff and sounds them again for reinforcement. The student can set the speed of dictation by touching the "speed" box or ask to hear an example again by touching the box marked "play again." The melody program also includes options for entering notes in solfeggio symbols or by touching a keyboard like the one shown in Figure 2.

Figure 2
Sample display from the GUIDO Melody Program

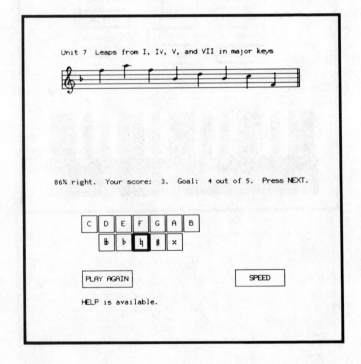

Chord Qualities

A sample display from the chord quality program is shown in Figure 3. GUIDO plays a chord and asks the student to touch both the quality and the inversion. By touching control boxes at the bottom of the screen, the students can hear the notes of the chord played again, make GUIDO pause while they study a chord; change the modes of presentation to make the notes of the chord play up, down, or simultaneously; and change the length of time the chords are played. When a student gets the correct answer, GUIDO reinforces it by writing the notes of the chord on the staff in the middle of the screen.

Figure 3
Sample display from the GUIDO Chord Quality Program

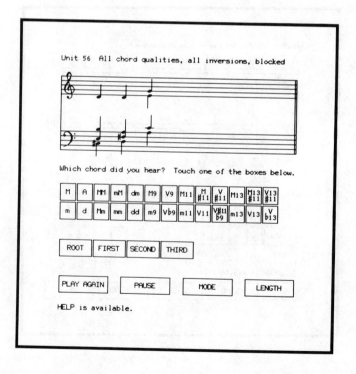

Harmonies

Figure 4 shows a sample display from the harmony program. GUIDO plays a four-part harmonic exercise in chorale style, and the student answers by touching Roman numerals and soprano and bass notes. As each note and Roman numeral is correctly answered, GUIDO writes it on the staff in notation. The student can change the speed of dictation or ask to hear the example played again. The student can also change the volume of each of the four voices, thereby making it easier to hear the individual lines of the chorale. This lesson in particular shows the great benefit of using the touch panel for answering oral questions; a complicated symbol that could be cumbersome and time-consuming to type on a typewriter keyset can be made by just touching a few boxes.

Figure 4
Sample display from the GUIDO Harmony Program

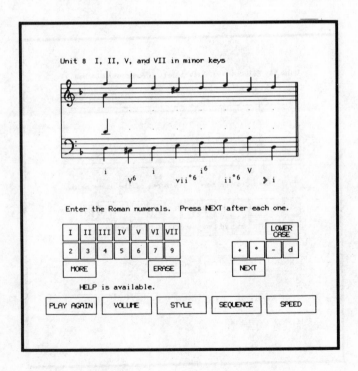

Rhythms

Figure 5 shows a sample display from the rhythm program. GUIDO plays a rhythm, and the student touches the boxes that correspond to the note values that were played. GUIDO displays each note value as the student gets it right. Again, the student has the option of changing the speed of dictation and of hearing the rhythm repeated. As with all of the GUIDO programs, the rhythm program is able to handle many levels of difficulty, from the simplest rhythms using combinations of full beat values to complex rhythms employing irregular divisions and tied notes.

Figure 5
Sample display from the GUIDO Rhythm Program

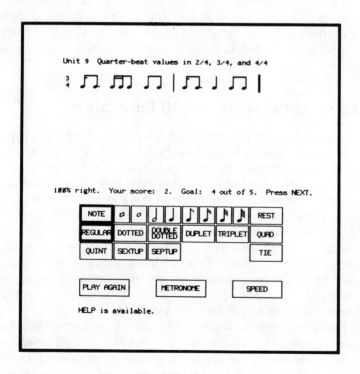

Instructor Options

A lot happens behind the scenes in the micro GUIDO ear-training system. The students receive individual courses of instruction; since they do not see the instruction received by other students, it would seem as if all of the programming work that went into GUIDO was done just for them as individuals. Actually, the programs are capable of being adjusted by the instructors for use by students varying in abilities from young children through advanced collegiate music majors.

The key to GUIDO's flexibility is its table-driven program design. Each GUIDO program reads a set of instructional variables from a master table. These variables tell the program what questions to ask, how to ask them, and what actions to take based on student performance. The master table can be changed easily by the instructor, who can create more than one table in order to apply different treatments to different groups of students. The micro GUIDO system comes with competency tables that have been carefully researched over the past seven years in order to provide the best sequencing of instruction. Most instructors simply use the tables that come with the system, although an instructor who wanted to change one of the units could do so by simply typing a different value into a table. No knowledge of computer programming is required to do this; instructors can even add totally new units to the curriculum.

The Extent of the Micro GUIDO Curriculum

The tables that are provided with the system represent a complete two-year course of study in ear-training. The average completion time of students going through this curriculum is 56 hours.

There are 27 interval units. Ascending intervals are presented first, and after students learn how to discriminate among just a few intervals, more and more intervals are added until all ascending intervals are drilled in the same unit. A similar strategy is then followed for descending intervals, and then harmonic intervals are covered. After the students have learned all of their ascending, descending, and harmonic intervals, compound intervals are introduced, following the same strategy. The intervals curriculum culminates in a unit that combines all simple and compound intervals.

The melody program begins with scalewise patterns. Short melodies and then longer melodies are dictated first in major and then in minor keys, and then triadic leaps are gradually introduced. Leaps of a sixth and seventh are studied, and then modulations are covered, first to closely related keys, and then to more distant keys. The melody units become increasingly more chromatic, and impressionistic and atonal patterns are practiced. Units on modal melodies and 12-tone rows are also included. There are 32 melody units in all.

The chord quality program can teach not only major, minor, augmented, and diminished triads in root position and in all inversions, but also dominant and nondominant seventh, ninth, eleventh, and thirteenth chords. The strategy followed in the chord quality program is similar to that of the intervals program. The curriculum begins with major and minor chords in root position. When the students master these, other qualities are added until all of the triads are asked. Then the inversions are added until the student can do all of the triads in all inversions. Seventh, ninth, eleventh, and thirteenth chords are gradually introduced using the same technique. There are 57 units of instruction in chord qualities.

The harmony units begin with the discrimination of tonic and dominant triads in root position. Subdominant, leading tone, supertonic, submediant, and mediant chords are progressively added until the students can hear exercises that call on all of the basic triads. Both major and minor modes are covered, with first inversion chords introduced along with the leading tone triad. After the students master root position and first inversion chords, second inversion chords are introduced, followed by the dominant seventh and its inversions. Diminished seventh chords and nondominant seventh chords are introduced, followed by secondary dominants, augmented sixth chords, Neapolitans, dominant ninth, eleventh, and thirteenth chords, and raised supertonic and submediant diminished seventh chords. In all there are 34 units of harmonic dictation.

Rhythmic dictation begins with undivided beat values in simple time. Divisions, subdivisions, and syncopations are covered, and then compound time is introduced with its divisions, subdivisions, and syncopations. Tied notes become increasingly more frequent throughout the curriculum, and duplets, triplets, and various irregular divisions of the beat are introduced. There are 40 units of rhythmic dictation.

Student Record Keeping

When students enter one of the GUIDO programs, they are shown a list of units. Each time a student completes a GUIDO unit, micro PLATO writes a star next to that unit on the student's floppy disk. Instructors can look at these completion stars throughout a course in order to track student progress in the curriculum. At the end of a course, the instructor can use a special option that erases the completion stars so that the disks can be used again by other students.

Changing Timbres

The University of Delaware Sound Synthesizer (UDSS) is fully programmable in the domains of frequency and time. The UDSS has 32 harmonics for each of its four voices, which are optionally expandable to eight voices. Tremolos and vibratos can be made by means of amplitude and frequency modulation, respectively. Glissandos and portamenti can be defined, and programmable memories are included to permit real-time performance controls.

An orchestration program has been designed whereby students can easily change the instrumentation of the UDSS. They can also make up their own ensembles, and they can even create their own instrument consisting of a waveform, an amplitude envelope, a frequency envelope, and a glissando factor. Students can use waveforms and envelopes that have been predefined by others, or they can make up their own. The use of the University of Delaware Sound Synthesizer to simulate orchestral sounds has greatly added to the realism of the computer-based music learning environment.

The micro GUIDO ear-training system is available from the University of Delaware. Persons interested in demonstrations, pricing information, and copies of the articles listed in the bibliography can request them by writing to the Office of Computer-Based Instruction, University of Delaware, Main and Academy Streets, Newark, Delaware 19711.

References

Hofstetter, Fred T. "Computer-Based Aural Training: The GUIDO System." *Journal of Computer-Based Instruction* 7(1981): 84–92.

Hofstetter, Fred T. "Music Dream Machines: New Realities for Computer-Based Music Instruction." *Creative Computing* III (March–April 1977): 50–54.

Hofstetter, Fred T. "Instructional Design and Curricular Impact of Computer-Based Music Education." *Educational Technology* 18 (April 1978): 50–53.

Hofstetter, Fred T. "Evaluation of a Competency-Based Approach to Teaching Aural Interval Identification." *Journal of Research in Music Education* 27 (1979): 201–213.

Hofstetter, Fred T. "Computer-Based Recognition of Perceptual Patterns in Harmonic Dictation Exercises." Proceedings of the 1978 ADCIS Conference, Dallas, Texas. Also in *Journal of Research in Music Education* 26 (1978): 111–119.

Hofstetter, Fred T. "Computer-Based Recognition of Perceptual Patterns in Chord Quality Dictatioɪ. Exercises." *Journal of Research in Music Education* 28 (1980): 83–91.

Hofstetter, Fred T. "Computer-Based Recognition of Perceptual Patterns and Learning Styles in Rhythmic Dictation Exercises." *Journal of Research in Music Education* 29 (1981): 265–278.

Hofstetter, Fred T. "Applications of the GUIDO System to Aural Skills Research." *College Music Symposium* 21 (Fall 1981): 46–53.

Hofstetter, Fred T. "The Sixth Summative Report of the Office of Computer-Based Instruction," ERIC Document, July 1981.

VII. Into the Future

22. Issues and Implications

M. Tim Grady

IN THE PRECEDING SECTIONS OF THIS BOOKLET WE HAVE ATTEMPTED TO describe how microcomputers have been and are being used in schools in the United States. Other examples exist, and more will exist soon. Key issues of staff development, research, and instructional planning have been discussed here. We in ASCD face these and other issues as we move toward a computer literate society. Let us review key issues that the competent curriculum leader must address in the '80s.

Issue 1: Teacher and Curriculum Staff Literacy

As discussed in Part IV, this need is critical to the success of a district's use of computers in schools. We must speak a common language, and we must stay up professionally with current hardware and software developments. School districts must design and implement staff development programs that are longitudinal in nature and depend on their own personnel for execution. Dependence on outside consultants will prove too costly and difficult for most districts.

Issue 2: Integration of Computers in Existing Curricula

State agencies and curriculum organizations must provide leadership in the areas of goals and objectives. Curriculum and instruction personnel must demand that state agencies provide a plan; without one, progress in curriculum integration will be piecemeal. Teachers are in need of examples of how others have integrated computer-assisted instruction with traditional curricula. This publication has, in part, been an effort to meet this need. ASCD members should share their knowledge in this area at meetings and in articles.

Issue 3: Research

Not only do we need empirical research on the effects of CAI and CMI on student achievement and attitudes, we also need research on effective presentation of computer-based curricula. We know little about graphics and sound. We are just beginning to explore sequencing and branching techniques. Before curriculum and instruction professionals become too biased in their evaluations of software, much more meaningful research needs to be carried out.

Issue 4: Hardware Obsolescence

At present, many schools are using or beginning to use hardware that, for the most part, is a variation or refinement of first-generation personal computers. That is, most use a single processor such as a 6502 or Z80. Most have a 40-column CRT or attach to a TV type monitor. These computers have small amounts of memory (that is, 8-32K usable) and are single user machines. Shortly these machines will be obsolete. The next generation will be multiuser, multitask systems that operate at faster speeds, have large memories, and employ multiple processors. Per-unit costs will come down and capability will increase. School leaders must come to grips with this situation within the next four years. Teachers can expect to have classroom sets of computers that are about the size of a three-ring notebook, use flat screen video displays, and need no floppy disks.

By the late '80s work stations acting as stand-alone systems or tapping large data bases will be interconnected via inexpensive telecommunication equipment (not telephones) and satellites. Each school will have access to "all" good software, and the idea of each school selecting and purchasing their own programs will seem incredulous to the curriculum planner of the '90s. We should do our present planning with an eye to the future.

Issue 5: Attitudes

Computers are an integral part of our society, yet there are educators who refuse to attend to this fact. Our society is engulfed in an information explosion, and managing information is what computers do best. Schools, in order to make realistic and effective use of computers, must employ computers as information managers. Our attitude toward the computer should be one of recognition of its power as an information system. Computers are more than programable teaching machines. The modern school leader needs to think positively about integrating computers into schools.

We who work in schools and who study ways to improve curriculum and instruction must work very hard to learn to use computers effectively. Our jobs are no longer well-defined. Some amount of planning, research, trial and error, argument, creativity, frustration, success, and refinement are ahead of us. Let us proceed.

23. The Little Red Computer in 2011: A Scenario

Michael C. Hynes and Nancy R. McGee

YAWNING, MILDRED HANOVER-BROWN RUBBED THE SLEEP FROM HER EYES AND, still only half awake, did what she did every morning before getting out of bed. She switched on the terminal that sat on her bedside table and focused on the day's immediate concerns.

MAY 14, 2011

IT IS 8:00 A.M. WEATHER: 18 CELSIUS AND FAIR SKIES.

YOU HAVE:

REMINDERS:
A) SEND FLOWERS, AUNT EDITH'S BIRTHDAY
B) HAIRDRESSER'S APPOINTMENT, 3:30 P.M. TODAY
C) RETIREMENT DINNER, 7:00 P.M., COMMUNITY CENTER

3 PIECES OF MAIL

3 USERS ON LINE:
A) MR. JONES, PRINCIPAL, USER # 857-24-0000
B) MRS. GREENE, DEPT. CHAIR, USER # 678-59-1342
C) HENRY DAVIS, PLUMBER, USER # 365-50-6843

3 STUDENT MESSAGES:
A) LILLY REQUESTS TEST # 753, USER # 5683-32-5911
B) GEORGE REQUESTS CONFERENCE, USER # 5016-97-4001
C) MARCY NEEDS AUTHORIZATION FOR NIXON DATA BASE, FILE 017, USER # 5423-57-8444

WHICH DO YOU WANT?

163

"Well, I'm certainly not in the mood for the plumber just yet," Mildred thought to herself, now fully awake and remembering her cantakerous water heater. She relegated Henry Davis' message to the lowest priority.

"Lilly will be in her usual state of pre-test jitters, so I'd better get her started on the exam right away." Quickly keying in Lilly's user number and her own all-important teacher identification number to the Scholastic Research and Testing Institute, Mildred authorized Lilly's access to Test 753, Analysis of Geopolitical Changes on the African Continent, 1990–2010. She followed this with a memo to George, setting his conference for 1:00 p.m. "That should give me time to get across town for my hair appointment at 3:30," she thought. "However, knowing George, I should get a confirmation on this.

"Let's see, Marcy is about finished with her comparison of the Nixon and Roosevelt tapes for her paper on the origins of electronic eavesdropping in government. Fifteen minutes on-line should be sufficient."

```
555-831-2619
ACCESS NUMBER?
4029
LIBRARY OF CONGRESS DATA BASE?
NIXON FILE 017
USER NUMBER?
5423-57-8444
CONFIRM—THIS IS A STUDENT NUMBER?
YES
ACCOUNT NUMBER?
895-75-2892
TIME LIMIT? (IN MINUTES)
15 MINUTES
```

As she completed Marcy's authorization sequence, Mildred noticed a flashing star in the upper right hand corner of the screen, which indicated an incoming message return.

```
CALL RETURN MESSAGE
HI, MS. H-B. SEE YOU AT ONE. GEORGE.

STATUS
IT IS 8:15 A.M. WEATHER: 19 CELSIUS AND FAIR SKIES.
```

"8:15. Better get up. I can take care of the rest of these messages after breakfast. Guess I should locate my employment data disk before getting on-line with Mr. Jones. Must have left it in the den." With that, Mildred switched off the machine and padded toward the shower.

```
STATUS
IT IS 9:00 A.M. WEATHER: 20 CELSIUS AND FAIR SKIES.
LOAD EMPLOYMENT DATA
READY
RUN
EMPLOYMENT DATA—MILDRED HANOVER–BROWN
INITIAL EMPLOYMENT: SEPTEMBER 5, 1981
REQUESTED RETIREMENT: MAY 4, 2011
```

"Okay. Now let's see what Mr. Jones has on his mind."

```
MESSAGE
PLEASE SUPPLY DATA RE 1983–84 LEAVE.
```

"Good morning, Junior," Mildred typed. "I know you're too young to remember, but some of us were forced to take maternity leave back in the '80s since teaching in those days required one's presence in the classroom on a daily basis. As you will note if you check some older records, this type of leave was fully credited toward retirement. By the way, when can I expect my cash settlement for unused sick leave to be credited to my account?"

Mildred sat back in her chair and took a slow sip of her steaming coffee. Now working from the terminal in her den, Mildred gazed through the window at a cloudless sky, her thoughts turning to Betty Greene. "She's been so considerate throughout this transition period. I would never have agreed to a retirement dinner if she hadn't been in charge of arrangements. I can trust her not to do something maudlin."

```
                        MESSAGE
GOOD MORNING, SOON-TO-BE LADY OF LEISURE.
PICK UP YOU AT 6:30 P.M.
REUP STATUS:  67 ATTENDING DINNER
              100 REQUESTED ELECTRONIC COMMUNICATION DURING
              PROGRAM. 14 SELECTED
              86 MESSAGES TRANSFERRED
WEAR YOUR RED DRESS
```

"Good grief!" One hundred people from around the world still remember old H-B. I just hope I remember them. Oh, I'd better notify Betty about the reassigning status of my students. Since she's the chair of the Social Studies Department, she'll need to evaluate the new teacher-student assignments soon. I think George, Lilly, and Marcy are the last."

RETURN MESSAGE

TO?
8679-59-1342
FROM?
895-75-2892
MESSAGE
ALL STUDENTS REASSIGNED EXCEPT GEORGE, 5016-97-4001; LILLY, 568-32-5911; MARCY, 5423-57-8444. WILL TRANSFER ALL RECORDS BY 5:00 P.M. TODAY. FINAL SESSION WITH GEORGE AT ONE.

The morning slipped by quickly and it was nearly noon by the time Mildred had finished grading papers. "Now to enter the grades," Mildred sighed, "and I'm ready to close my records." She quickly keyed in the figures and authorized their release to the Student Accountability Network.

"Just time for a bite to eat before George arrives." As Mildred moved into the kitchen to prepare a salad for lunch, she thought regretfully of the days ahead with no print-outs to grade, no student messages to answer, no discussion groups to coordinate, and no conferences to schedule.

"I wonder what George will do when he's used all his educational vouchers. He's so dependent on others and hardly ever completes a task without numerous conferences to make sure he's proceeding correctly. If only he could . . . well, at least he's better off than the 'Georges' of fifteen or twenty years ago. They were the faceless ones in the old centralized schools. It was easy to get lost in a class of 30 to 40 students. I sometimes find it hard to believe that I started teaching in a system where the teacher presented a myriad of facts to the group by lecture enhanced with the old overhead projector, and all students were expected to grasp the material. Our 'Georges' in the class, of course, learned very little. They needed individualized programs and interactive situations such as group discussions. Most importantly, they needed time for reflective thinking. Thank goodness the educational system can now respond to the need of the 'Georges' of the world. I don't know what would have happened to this George if we hadn't been able to diagnose his learning style accurately and constantly monitor his progress. Once we identified his aptitude for visual learning, the interactive video program made a real difference—at least in social studies."

The doorbell chimed imperiously. "Oh, that's George now and I haven't done my lunch dishes. Well, from now on there will be plenty of time for cleaning.

"Hi, George, come on into the den. I'll be with you in a moment."

Mildred and George were deep in discussion when the buzzer on the den console interrupted them some time later.

> **STATUS**
> IT IS 3:04 P.M. WEATHER: 21 CELSIUS AND FAIR SKIES.
> DON'T FORGET YOUR HAIR APPOINTMENT.

As George was leaving for the last time, Mildred was struck with the finality of his exit, but couldn't keep herself from her usual reminder. "George, if you need any further help, you know you can call me."

"Don't worry, Ms. Hanover-Brown. You know how hard it is to get rid of me," George called as he waved farewell.

"Darn! I'm running late. Better hurry." Once in the car, Mildred accessed her mobile terminal mounted in the dashboard.

> **STATUS**
> IT IS 3:15 P.M. WEATHER: 21 CELSIUS AND FAIR SKIES.
> TRAFFIC STATUS?
> YES
> DESTINATION?
> WESTSIDE: BEAUMONT STREET
> NO DETOURS, NO CONSTRUCTION BETWEEN ELM AND BEAUMONT STREETS.
> MESSAGE TO MARSHA'S HAIR SALON: 505-368-5328
> LEAVING HOME NOW. MAY BE A FEW MINUTES LATE. MILDRED H-B.
> SEND

Making her way across town, Mildred passed Goodyear High School, her former teaching station before the implementation of the educational voucher system.

"There's Goodyear. I hate to think how many students were processed through that facility. So many faces; so many stories. The student loads were so large I can't remember them all, though some come to mind quickly. If it weren't for Mary Heddens, my retirement party would certainly be different. She was one of the first of the new generation of students—a very independent learner who knew how to capitalize on the power and flexibility of computer learning. It helped that her parents set up one of the first home computer learning stations. To think it's only been 20 years since students began to access data bases from universities and research institutes, take part in computerized tours from the Metropolitan Museum in New York, the Smithsonian, and even attend the Boston Pops concerts via CRT. Mary did all of these and sought more and more opportunities. And today she's famous for her work in transmitting holographs. I was thrilled to hear that she volunteered to arrange for me to visit 'live' with fourteen of my former students tonight. There's Marsha's. I wonder how late I am?"

STATUS
IT IS 3:34 P.M. WEATHER: 21 CELSIUS AND FAIR SKIES.

The hairdresser's salon was busy as usual. "Do you mind waiting a few minutes, Mildred?" Marsha asked. "I am just finishing Mrs. Simpson."

"That's fine, I'll sit here and chat with her while you work. I've just been winding up my work with her daughter Lilly today. She's one of my last students."

"Hello, Mrs. Simpson. Did Lilly finish her test?"

"Well, I think so. She was still at the terminal when I left, but she seemed to be about ready to print your copy. She certainly is going to miss you. You've been so patient with her, and I feel that the African Project you directed was really instrumental in her decision."

"What decision?"

"Oh, I thought she had talked with you about it. I guess you've noticed that Lilly is a sensitive girl. Of our three children, she has always been the most concerned with social problems. When her brother wants to be a tease, he delights in calling her 'the great humanitarian.' Anyway, she's decided to trade her remaining educational access vouchers to finance a field study. Using the voucher credit to pay transportation and support, she's going to work for the next six months in a World Hunger Crisis Zone in Ghabia."

"How wonderful!" exclaimed Mildred. "On the one hand, I hate to hear that she's leaving the network—I guess I never feel that they've learned all we have to offer. But on the other hand, I know Lilly isn't going to be satisfied until she gets in the field and works directly with some of the problems we've investigated. Lilly has so much to offer. I'm sure she'll be an asset in the hunger zone."

"Well, as her mother, I naturally have some reservations about her ending her public education now—not to mention her being so far from home."

"Let me see," mused Mildred, "I believe I have another former student currently working in the Ghabian Hunger Zone. I'll check the network files and get Ned's exact location. Perhaps her meeting someone else from Fairfield would ease both your minds."

"It certainly would be a relief to me. I'll tell Lilly to expect the message."

"Yes, and I'd like her to come and visit with me before she leaves. Although my teacher identification access number will be erased after tonight and I can't get to the expensive data bases, I should be able to help her locate some further information on the Ghabian situation through the free Public Access Bases. Besides I want to give her a hug and wish her well."

"Thanks, Ms. Hanover-Brown. I'll see that Lilly gets in touch. Looks like Marsha has done about all she can for me, so I'd better get going. Fred and I want to wish you all the best in your retirement."

"Thank you. 'Bye. Marsha, work a miracle on me. I want to look extra glamorous this evening."

STATUS
IT IS 11:17 P.M. WEATHER: 17 CELSIUS AND PARTLY CLOUDY.

DO YOU REQUIRE WAKE-UP?
NO
REMINDERS?
YES
SEND BETTY GREENE FLOWERS
SEND THANK-YOU MESSAGES
CALL HENRY DAVIS, PLUMBER

"Partly cloudy, my eye!" Mildred sighed as she kicked off her shoes and collapsed on her sofa. "All that work Marsha did on my hair, only to have it drenched in a sudden downpour." Yet she smiled to herself as she looked back on the hours so shortly passed. "What a night. I'm glad it's all on tape so I can relive it in my old age, which I am very much feeling right now.

"Of the hundreds of students I've taught, I can't believe Mary Heddens located the exact ones I wanted to see by holograph. It was so sweet of her to include Linda. I thought that daughter of mine was so deep in the jungle that not even the Archeological Location Network could find her. What a thrill to see her at the site and looking so terrific. I wish her father were alive to see her work; I really miss him on occasions like this." She thought reminiscently about the dinner. "I loved seeing Eric Freeman and his wife and new baby in his New York studio. Eric nearly drove me crazy with his stubborn refusal to do anything but paint. I'll never forget his telling me that he refused to spend another minute at his computer learning station. 'One becomes obsessed, Ms. Hanover-Brown,' he said, 'and I only have time for one obsession—painting.' " Mildred smiled. "Then the school district bought into the Worldwide Museum and Studio Data Base, and Eric nearly used up all his vouchers in a few weeks."

She thought of the other students who visited by holograph. "Imagine Paul Prouse, a judge, and Ellen Elizabeth Seay, a spacecraft pilot. I'm going to enjoy looking at the tape tomorrow and seeing them all again. Right now I'm too tired, and it's off to bed for Mildred."

She paused at the sight of her purse and the evening's memorabilia piled in a chair by the door. "But first, there's one thing I must do." She drew the small rectangular plaque from its wrappings, and removing the list of student numbers from over the bedside console, carefully hung the plaque and stepped back to read:

Because her love of learning, scholarship, and intellectual curiosity have been an inspiration to the students of Fairfield School District, The School Board hereby awards the lifetime use of Teacher Identification Number 895-75-2892 to Mildred Anne Hanover-Brown.

1981–2011

"Retirement is not termination."

STATUS
IT IS 11:45 P.M. WEATHER: 15 CELSIUS AND PARTLY CLOUDY.

ADD REMINDER
ACCESS INFO FROM CRUISESCHED: BRAZIL TOUR

END

About the Authors

M. Tim Grady
Director of Secondary Curriculum, Fort Campbell Dependent Schools; Fort Campbell, Kentucky.

Jane D. Gawronski
Assistant Superintendent for Educational Services and Programs, Walnut Valley Unified School District; Walnut, California.

Judith Edwards Allen
Director, Computer Technology Program, Northwest Regional Laboratory; Portland, Oregon.

Ronald E. Anderson
Minnesota Educational Computing Consortium; St. Paul, Minnesota.

Karen Billings
Manager, Instructional Computing, School Division, Houghton Mifflin Company; Boston, Massachusetts.

Ludwig Braun
Professor of Electrical Engineering and Software Director, Office of Instructional Development, New York Institute of Technology; Old Westbury, New York.

Kenneth E. Brumbaugh
Minnesota Educational Computing Consortium; St. Paul, Minnesota.

Donna M. Byrne
Systems Engineer, Software Tools, United Technologies, Norden Systems; Melville, New York.

Fred T. Hofstetter
Director of the Office of Computer-Based Instruction and Associate Professor of Music and Educational Studies, University of Delaware; Newark, Delaware.

Beverly Hunter
Senior Staff Scientist, Human Resources Research Organization; Alexandria, Virginia.

Lyndal R. Hutcherson
President, Texas Education Computer Association; Carrollton, Texas.

Michael C. Hynes
Professor of Education, Instructional Programs, University of Central Florida; Orlando, Florida.

Beverly J. Jones
Assistant Professor, Art Education Department, School of Architecture and Allied Arts, University of Oregon; Eugene, Oregon.

Paul Lorton, Jr.
Associate Professor of Information Systems, University of San Francisco; San Francisco, California.

Gerald Lundeen
Associate Professor, Graduate School of Library Studies, University of Hawaii; Honolulu, Hawaii.

Nancy R. McGee
Associate Professor, Instructional Programs, University of Central Florida; Orlando, Florida.

Eugene James Muscat
Director of Academic Services, University of San Francisco; San Francisco, California.

Donald Piele
Mathematics Department, University of Wisconsin—Parkside; Kenosha, Wisconsin.

James L. Poirot
Chairman, Computer Science Department, North Texas State University; Denton, Texas.

Sandra K. Pratscher
Education Specialist for Instructional Computing, Texas Education Agency; Austin, Texas.

Robert Shostak
Florida International University, Tamiami Campus; Miami, Florida.

Charlene E. West
Curriculum Coordinator, Math/Science, Cajun Valley Union School District; El Cajun, California.

Ramon Zamora
Electronic Education Specialist, Computertown USA! Palo Alto, California.

ASCD Publications, Spring 1983

Yearbooks

A New Look at Progressive Education
(610-17812) $8.00
Considered Action for Curriculum Improvement
(610-80186) $9.75
Education for an Open Society
(610-74012) $8.00
Feeling, Valuing, and the Art of Growing:
Insights into the Affective
(610-77104) $9.75
Fundamental Curriculum Decisions
(610-83290) $10.00
Improving the Human Condition
(610-78132) $9.75
Life Skills in School and Society
(610-17786) $5.50
Lifelong Learning—A Human Agenda
(610-79160) $9.75
Perceiving, Behaving, Becoming: A New Focus
for Education (610-17278) $5.00
Perspectives on Curriculum Development
1776-1976 (610-76078) $9.50
Schools in Search of Meaning
(610-75044) $8.50
Staff Development/Organization Development
(610-81232) $9.75
Supervision of Teaching (610-82262) $10.00

Books and Booklets

About Learning Materials (611-78134) $4.50
Adventuring, Mastering, Associating: New
Strategies for Teaching Children
(611-76080) $5.00
Applied Strategies for Curriculum Evaluation
(611-81240) $5.75
Approaches to Individualized Education
(611-80204) $4.75
Bilingual Education for Latinos
(611-78142) $6.75
Classroom-Relevant Research in the Language
Arts (611-78140) $7.50
Clinical Supervision—A State of the Art Review
(611-80194) $3.75
Computers in Curriculum and Instruction
(611-83292) $9.00
Curriculum Leaders: Improving Their Influence
(611-76084) $4.00
Curriculum Materials 1981 (611-81266) $3.00
Curriculum Materials 1982 (611-82268) $4.00
Curriculum Theory (611-77112) $7.00
Degrading the Grading Myths: A Primer of
Alternatives to Grades and Marks
(611-76082) $6.00
Developing Basic Skills Programs in
Secondary Schools (611-82264) $5.00
Developmental Characteristics of Children and
Youth (wall chart) (611-75058) $2.00
Developmental Supervision: Alternative
Practices for Helping Teachers Improve
Instruction (611-81234) $5.00
Educating English-Speaking Hispanics
(611-80202) $6.50
Educators' Challenge: Healthy Mothers,
Healthy Babies (611-81244) $4.00
Educators' Challenge Progressive Chart
(611-81252) $2.00
Effective Instruction (611-80212) $6.50
Elementary School Mathematics: A Guide to
Current Research (611-75056) $5.00
Eliminating Ethnic Bias in Instructional
Materials: Comment and Bibliography
(611-74020) $3.25
Global Studies: Problems and Promises for
Elementary Teachers (611-76086) $4.50
Handbook of Basic Citizenship Competencies
(611-80196) $4.75
Healthy Mothers—Healthy Babies
(611-81244) $4.00
Healthy Mothers—Healthy Babies (wall chart)
(611-81252) $2.00

Helping Teachers Manage Classrooms (611-
82266) $8.50
Humanistic Education: Objectives and
Assessment (611-78136) $4.75
Mathematics Education Research
(611-81238) $6.75
Measuring and Attaining the Goals of Education
(611-80210) $6.50
Middle School in the Making
(611-74024) $5.00
The Middle School We Need
(611-75060) $2.50
Moving Toward Self-Directed Learning
(611-79166) $4.75
Multicultural Education: Commitments, Issues,
and Applications (611-77108) $7.00
Needs Assessment: A Focus for Curriculum
Development (611-75048) $4.00
Open Education: Critique and Assessment
(611-75054) $4.75
Partners: Parents and Schools
(611-79168) $4.75
Preparing Your Curriculum Guide
(611-80208) $8.50
Professional Supervision for Professional
Teachers (611-75046) $4.50
Readings in Educational Supervision
(611-82272) $9.00
Readings on Curriculum Implementation
(611-80200) $4.00
Reschooling Society: A Conceptual Model
(611-17950) $2.00
The School of the Future—NOW
(611-17920) $3.75
Schools Become Accountable: A PACT
Approach (611-74016) $3.50
The School's Role as Moral Authority
(611-77110) $4.50
Selecting Learning Experiences: Linking
Theory and Practice (611-78138) $4.75
Social Studies for the Evolving Individual
(611-17952) $3.00
Social Studies in the 1980s
(611-82270) $8.75
Staff Development: Staff Liberation
(611-77106) $6.50
Supervision: Emerging Profession
(611-17796) $5.00
Supervision in a New Key (611-17926) $2.50
Urban Education: The City as a Living
Curriculum (611-80206) $6.50
Vitalizing the High School (611-74026) $3.50

Discounts on quantity orders of same title to
single address: 10-49 copies, 10%; 50 or more
copies, 15%. Make checks or money orders
payable to ASCD. Orders totaling $20.00 or
less must be prepaid. Orders from institutions
and businesses must be on official purchase
order form. Shipping and handling charges will
be added to billed purchase orders. *Please be
sure to list the stock number of each publication, shown in parentheses.*

Subscription to *Educational Leadership*—$18.00
a year. ASCD Membership dues: Regular (subscription [$18] and yearbook)—$38.00 a year;
Comprehensive (includes subscription [$18]
and yearbook plus other books and booklets
distributed during period of membership)—
$48.00 a year.

Order from:

Association for Supervision and
Curriculum Development
225 North Washington Street
Alexandria, Virginia 22314

0139